"Practical advice that will boost your brand visibility."

—Terry Nicholson, cofounder of PRAXIS S-10

"If you're really serious about growth, *Next Level Now* serves up the kind of sensible, no-holds-barred productive PR smarts that your business needs. Heather is the best in the biz. If you're willing to implement these tools she provides, you'll learn to work smarter than your competition."

—Andy Ryan, owner of HomeWorks Plumbing, Heating & Air

"Successful public relations create buzz. Buzz is what happens when people (not you) tell other people how amazing you are. Once you get some buzz going, it gets louder and can bring in massive numbers of customers. It may take some $$ to get it going, but once it's going, it's more powerful than marketing or advertising, and it doesn't cost anything. Pretty cool, right? Heather has taught me a lot about PR, and I'm delighted to create some buzz about her terrific, must-read new book, *Next Level Now*!"

—Ellen Rohr, president of Zoom Drain Franchise Company, LLC

NEXT
LEVEL
Now

HEATHER RIPLEY

NEXT LEVEL

Now

PR Secrets to Drive Explosive Growth for Your Home Service Business

Advantage®

Published by Advantage, Charleston, South Carolina.
Member of Advantage Media Group.

ADVANTAGE is a registered trademark, and the Advantage colophon is a trademark of Advantage Media Group, Inc.

Printed in the United States of America.

10 9 8 7 6 5 4 3 2 1

ISBN: 978-1-64225-230-9
LCCN: 2021901700

Cover and layout design by David Taylor.

This publication is designed to provide accurate and authoritative information in regard to the subject matter covered. It is sold with the understanding that the publisher is not engaged in rendering legal, accounting, or other professional services. If legal advice or other expert assistance is required, the services of a competent professional person should be sought.

 Advantage Media Group is proud to be a part of the Tree Neutral® program. Tree Neutral offsets the number of trees consumed in the production and printing of this book by taking proactive steps such as planting trees in direct proportion to the number of trees used to print books. To learn more about Tree Neutral, please visit **www.treeneutral.com**.

Advantage Media Group is a publisher of business, self-improvement, and professional development books and online learning. We help entrepreneurs, business leaders, and professionals share their Stories, Passion, and Knowledge to help others Learn & Grow. Do you have a manuscript or book idea that you would like us to consider for publishing? Please visit **advantagefamily.com** or call **1.866.775.1696**.

To my dad.

Thank you for teaching me to value a job well done and that every hard worker, no matter their title, deserves the same respect. You taught me to appreciate the skill in the skilled trades and not to expect everything in life to be handed to me. You are my hero, and I dedicate this book to you.

CONTENTS

FOREWORD

by Ara Mahdessian

When Heather approached me about writing the foreword to this book, I was delighted, because we share the same passion for supporting the home service industry.

All home service business owners have to evolve and think differently if they are going to grow their businesses. And that's not easy to do. I watched my dad work very long hours to solve various challenges in his small plumbing business. That's why Vahe Kuzoyan and I created ServiceTitan, to help give hardworking professionals like him the tools to succeed.

It's also why I'm so glad that Heather published *Next Level Now: PR Secrets to Drive Explosive Growth for Your Home Service Business.*

This book is a timely tool for your toolbox. You probably feel that your top challenge for growth is getting your phone to ring more (and it is extremely important). And no doubt, you understand the importance of marketing, or you wouldn't have picked up this book. What you might not understand is the power of PR to position you as the leading expert in your market and build your credibility, which over time helps you increase the pipeline for new business. Since very few understand the power of PR, it is an easy way to really stand out from your competitors.

In this book, Heather will share how to unleash the power of public relations to jumpstart your growth. Since she's been working with the industry for over a decade, she understands the unique challenges you have.

I have experienced the power of PR to grow businesses, and I hope you will use it to boost your brand awareness. The future success of your business starts now. All you have to do is turn the page.

Ara Mahdessian

Cofounder and CEO, ServiceTitan

by Tab Hunter

You're holding a true key to business growth in your hands. Heather's book comes at a time when the home service industry is facing unprecedented challenges, and her vision of how to put public relations to work for your business is essential for success in today's marketplace.

After experiencing the benefits of PR in the explosive growth of Tab Hunter Plumbing, my years in leadership at Clockwork Home Services, and now my latest venture, The Surfin' Plumbers, I am convinced that PR is a marketing secret that contractors must put to work to grow and thrive. The marketing landscape has changed dramatically over the years, and now more than ever, successful contractors must do things differently in order to stand out from the competition and dominate the markets they serve.

Years ago, when Heather worked for me at Clockwork Home Services, she was an integral part of our franchise development success and helped position the company for acquisition. Even during the height of the Great Recession, Clockwork was selling and awarding new franchise territories in record numbers, largely due to our focus on PR.

Heather has a unique ability to turn my thirty-thousand-foot vision into a clear, actionable plan, so when it came time to launch The Surfin' Plumbers, I turned to her to create a concrete and effective public relations strategy that set the stage for massive growth.

Consumers want instant access to information about the companies they choose to work with. Old-fashioned word of mouth isn't so old-fashioned anymore, as online reviews can build or harm your reputation. In this new world, relying on the same old tired marketing tactics just won't cut it. Instead, allow Heather to show you what it takes to thrive in these competitive times, now and in the future, through the use of strategic public relations.

Knowing how to leverage PR can be instrumental in your journey toward financial freedom and success. So, get ready to learn the PR secrets that, if you commit to their implementation, will help your company reach its maximum potential. The results will be worth it. Of course, you probably already realize this, or you wouldn't have picked up this book.

Tab Hunter
President, The Surfin' Plumbers

Does Public Relations Really Work?

The next opportunity can be yours.

The next opportunity to tell your company's story, to highlight your services, to demonstrate your expertise.

It can be your plumbing company on the local news, instructing viewers how to prepare for the next deep freeze. It can be your heating and air conditioning company, quoted in a newspaper or magazine article on strategies homeowners can use to save energy.

If you own a residential service business, you have probably seen your competitors on the local news and wondered how they did it. Why did the news station call them instead of you, especially if you're spending thousands of dollars in advertising with them?

How does a company like One Hour Heating & Air Conditioning become a known industry and household name? What did it do that other service businesses did not?

I want you to have these kinds of opportunities—opportunities that will translate into name recognition, new customers, and the ability to grow your business. The secret to generating these opportunities is public relations. And it's a secret that I want to share with you.

I know that there are a lot of books out there, many of which focus on how to use marketing to get better results for your business. I have read quite a few of them myself! As the owner of a recognized and highly regarded service industry public relations agency, I regularly read books on marketing to learn from and stay on top of industry trends and to make sure that our agency is offering the best and highest level of expertise to our clients.

But this book is not just another how-to manual on marketing or public relations. This book is written specifically for you, and for all the residential service business owners who want to learn how to implement public relations strategies into their marketing campaigns and take their business to the next level. I've seen it happen countless times with my clients. Public relations is a key strategy they can use to develop a competitive advantage. It's effective, it's smart—and it's likely that your competitors aren't using it.

I've worked with home service businesses for over a decade, including brands like One Hour Heating & Air Conditioning, helping people like you leverage the power of earned media to increase your credibility in the market, hire and retain the best technicians, and make the phone ring.

I've chosen to specialize in the home service industry because I have tremendous respect for the work you do. I'm proud of the fact that my company, Ripley PR, is the number one PR agency in the home service space, and that so many of my clients are experts in heating and air conditioning, plumbing, and electrical services.

But this book is intended to speak to more than just those three trades. If your business provides a skilled service to customers in their homes—whether it's roofing, window or garage door replacement, gutter repairs, or residential construction—the strategies I'll share will help your company grow.

By learning the ins and outs of public relations for service businesses from this book, you'll gain an insider's perspective on what the most practical aspects of PR are for you and which PR activities will get you the best return on your investment.

I care deeply about people like you. People who are skilled at making sure that customers are safe, comfortable, and healthy in their homes. I grew up in a blue-collar family. My father was an automotive collision technician (body man). My grandfather was a truck driver. My great-grandfather was an electrician for South Carolina Power & Light Company. It's important to me to be able to help business owners like you. You're family.

Think of this book as your guidebook to implementing PR for your service business the best way, the most effective way, and most importantly the right way. There are many PR pitfalls that service businesses can fall prey to. My goal in this book is to inform and guide you through the eyes of an expert. I hope you will find this book helpful and begin implementing as many suggestions as you can, and at least bookmark other chapters for future use.

WHY PR MATTERS

I titled this introduction with a question: Does public relations really work? Let me answer that question by sharing a story—a story that explains why I'm passionate about what I do.

My first job in the home service industry was for a company called Clockwork Home Services. Clockwork was the parent company of three successful franchise brands, and I was hired to manage marketing in what was very much a dream job, creating branding and marketing campaigns for the company's brands: One Hour Heating & Air Conditioning, Benjamin Franklin Plumbing, and Mister Sparky. My goal was to build on the already strong reputation of these three franchise companies to support the effort to sell franchises to contractors.

One of the first lessons I learned was the value of a nationally recognized franchise name. If you've built a successful independent business with your name on the door, it can be challenging to sell that business when you're ready to retire. A franchise brand name creates an enduring presence—it enables your business (and its reputation) to extend beyond one man or woman.

Since I was responsible for managing marketing, my job was to help explain the value of owning a franchise to contractors through our messaging—to interest someone who, for example, had a successful plumbing business to consider converting to a franchise, change their company name and rebrand everything, and implement the steps to build and grow their business.

I developed tremendous respect for the professionals involved in these three trades. And I began to recognize that what I liked best— what I was successful at—was creating public relations strategies to support the business owners.

One day, my senior management at Clockwork came to me and explained that, after years of helping small business owners create plans to cement their legacies, the CEO was thinking about his own. He was ready to retire and sell the business. He wanted to attract a large company, one big enough to buy not one or two of the franchise brands, but all of them. To do that, he wanted to develop a public relations campaign big enough to get national attention.

We brainstormed some ideas—we even joked about how great it would be if you were watching a show like *Desperate Housewives* and one of our branded trucks pulled up in the background of a scene.

It was a crazy idea, but I kept coming back to it. How did that particular brand of chips end up on the table in a sitcom family's kitchen? Why was an actor driving that specific make of car during a dramatic chase?

I knew nothing about product placement when I started, but I quickly learned that there is nothing random about a product or brand earning that kind of visibility. It's all part of a careful strategy. Every brand that you see in a TV show or movie—they worked hard to get that placement.

After a lot of research, I recognized that the reality show *The Celebrity Apprentice* presented a great opportunity to profile the company and franchisees in a way that would create the kind of national buzz the CEO was hoping for.

When I first recommended this strategy, some of our executives admitted they had never watched this show, so I bought a season on DVD and shared it. Everyone loved the idea.

I worked hard to create a pitch that would appeal to the show's producers. The press kit I sent them featured 8 × 10 photos of the colorful trucks and our service experts and highlighted the fact that the technicians were all clean-cut, wore neatly professional uniforms, and were carefully screened with felony background checks and drug testing. The producers were intrigued by my pitch, but initially expressed interest in only featuring one of our franchise brands.

This, of course, was precisely the opposite of what the CEO wanted. His goal was to make sure that all our brands were promoted equally. So we went back to the producers and continued negotiating until they agreed to feature all three brands in the episode.

It was a huge success. There was so much interest that the company's websites crashed the day after the episode aired. And a few months later, the CEO was able to sell the company, just as he had hoped.

You may not need that kind of national campaign. You may need a strategy that's more targeted, building brand awareness through local media. You may want to cement your reputation as an industry expert or leverage that expertise to franchise your business, create more effective media appearances, or better respond to competition in your market.

No matter your goal, no matter your specific trade, public relations can help you grow your business to the next level.

GET PREPARED

In the pages that follow, I'll share proven strategies that have helped my clients increase their credibility in the market and leverage that credibility into more customers and more revenue. We'll start by discussing exactly what PR is—and what it isn't. I'll explain the difference between PR and advertising and marketing so that you clearly understand how each plays a key role in your communication strategy.

Next, I'll guide you through a strategic analysis of your business from a PR perspective, focusing on the critical aspects of strengths, weaknesses, opportunities, and threats—or SWOT. This SWOT analysis will equip you with an in-depth understanding of how best to harness PR to grow your businesses. I'll offer insights into how to assess your competition, leading you through a careful analysis of what the competition is doing right and where their actions have created opportunities for you and your business.

With this clear picture of your competitive landscape, you'll be positioned to create a meaningful PR strategy. I'll show you how to develop a social media plan that is targeted, engaging, and impactful.

I'll explain the steps you can take to ensure that your website is converting viewers into customers. Together, we'll craft a PR plan that cements your reputation as an expert in your market, and I'll share my proven media training techniques to increase your comfort—and your visibility.

Because crises can happen, I'll discuss how to respond swiftly and effectively to protect your brand and your reputation. Finally, I'll share insights that will help you identify how and when to partner with a specialist, ensuring that you optimize your PR dollars.

If you follow the PR practices set out in the following chapters and commit to actively making these practices a part of your business plan, it will help you grow from an average service business to a multi-million-dollar industry leader. It's your business. I can help you build it into the next household name.

NEXT
LEVEL
NOW

CHAPTER ONE

Why You Need a PR Strategy

"I don't need public relations—that's for big companies and companies with an image problem." "I'll worry about PR when my company is bigger." "I already have a marketing plan that's working."

Sound familiar? I've heard versions of these statements from far too many home service businesses. But the reality is this: every business, no matter the size, can benefit from a thoughtful, well-executed PR strategy. If you follow the guidelines I'll outline in this book, you'll discover that a small commitment of time will pay off in a significantly increased awareness of your business. And while each can support the other, marketing and public relations are not interchangeable—they play a unique and specific role in supporting growth and increasing awareness of your brand and your business.

So, let's start with two simple questions:

What is PR? And why does your home service business need it to break through to the next level?

When I talk about PR, I of course mean public relations, and I'll use both the full term and its abbreviation in this book. Public relations, at its core, is about using strategic communication to build relationships between your business and the public you serve.

In PR, it's not just about what you are doing right; what you are not doing also matters.

Most of the great home service businesses, including residential heating and air conditioning experts, plumbers, electricians, landscapers, and window replacement contractors, understand the importance of really good marketing to help bring in more business. But what is public relations? And how does it differ from advertising or marketing or branding?

> **Public relations, at its core, is about using strategic communication to build relationships between your business and the public you serve.**

Proactive public relations can help your service business grow by positioning you as the leading expert in your market. Unlike most traditional marketing tactics, PR can offer a true competitive advantage for your business because most of your competitors won't be using it. It can also be a critical resource in the event of a crisis, providing strategic support to help you respond effectively when the reputation of your business is threatened.

Let me share an illustration adapted from branding expert Marty Neumeier that will help explain the differences between marketing, branding, advertising, and public relations:[1]

---

1   Marty Neumeier, *The Brand Gap* (Berkeley, CA: New Riders, 2006).

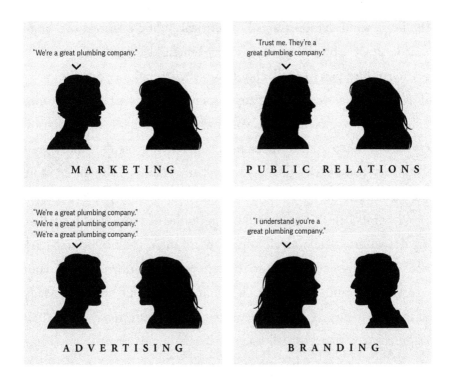

As you can see, in the first graphic, the man tells the woman, "We're a great plumbing company." That's a marketing message. He's conveying the message about himself that he wants her to know. Just below, he says to her, "We're a great plumbing company. We're a great plumbing company. We're a great plumbing company." That's advertising. He's using repetition to reinforce his message. Repetition can be very effective for creating top-of-mind awareness. In the next image (top right), another woman, a third party, says to the woman, "Trust me. They're a great plumbing company." That's public relations—getting a third party to talk about you. Finally, we get the payoff of these combined strategies, which in Neumeier's illustration is labeled as a branding success: the woman says, "I understand you're a great plumbing company."

Effective, strategic communication depends on a multifaceted approach, involving marketing, advertising, and public relations. And the illustration demonstrates how critical public relations can be to that kind of a branding campaign. Remember, public relations is getting a third party to talk about you, your brand, or your company. If an individual—or a company—spends a lot of time and money telling you how great they are, you may understandably be a bit suspicious. But when another person or source confirms that message—"Yes, they really are as great as they claim to be"—you will be more inclined to listen.

My focus in this book will be on public relations, but before we dig deeper into that strategic approach, I think it's helpful to step back and take a big-picture view of the role public relations plays in your efforts to communicate with clients and grow your business. Many of the companies I talk to believe that they are effectively using their resources to accomplish all four—marketing, advertising, branding, and public relations. I have the unpleasant task of explaining that they are focusing only on one—generally advertising or marketing—and neglecting the opportunity to harness all four to achieve their goals. Here are some more detailed definitions of marketing, advertising, branding, and public relations. All are equally important in taking your business to the next level in credibility and revenue growth.

MARKETING

According to the American Marketing Association, "Marketing is the activity, set of institutions, and processes for creating, communicating, delivering, and exchanging offerings that have value for customers, clients, partners, and society at large."[2] So what does that really mean? Marketing, as a general term, includes everything your business does

---

2   American Marketing Association, "Definitions of Marketing," accessed November 24, 2020, https://www.ama.org/the-definition-of-marketing-what-is-marketing/.

to encourage customers to buy your product or service. Think about the illustration I shared earlier: one person telling another person how great their plumbing company is. In simplified terms, that's marketing. Your marketing—the message you share about your business or service—comes from you, not from other people.

ADVERTISING

Advertising is often a part of an overall marketing plan. Effective marketers will research and evaluate which advertising channels will offer the most bang for the buck, then implement an advertising campaign, and analyze the metrics to evaluate if the advertising was effective. What do I mean by "analyze the metrics"? A *metric* is a way to measure success—in this case, the success of an advertising campaign. Did more people book appointments, visit your website, or request a particular service after an advertising campaign? Those are great metrics.

For home service businesses, advertising usually consists of paid print, direct mail, radio ads, TV spots, truck wraps, billboards, signage, and other paid media. Think back to the illustration—the man repeating how great his company is, over and over. That's frequently the purpose of advertising: repeating the message so often that the consumer remembers it.

BRANDING

Branding goes hand in hand with marketing, advertising, and public relations. Branding is usually part of an overall marketing strategy, so that marketing activities using branding are consistent across all channels. The consumer often already has an opinion formed through effective branding. She knows what the other person's brand stands for and (in the illustration) repeats it to him for verification.

For home service businesses, branding will help differentiate your business from your competitors. Your brand—usually your company name, logo, truck wraps—should be unique and recognizable. It represents your business and acts as a kind of promise of what your customer can expect. Try this test: think of three different brands—maybe a brand of soda or snack food, an automobile brand, and a brand of athletic gear. Each of those brands suggests an image, an experience, an expectation.

You should have the same goal for your business. Your brand should immediately communicate something to your customer—about the quality of your work, the pricing, the skill and competence of your service.

PUBLIC RELATIONS

Finally, we get to the topic I'm most passionate about, the one I know will give you a real competitive advantage. Yes, public relations.

Let's look first at the definition of public relations shared by the Public Relations Society of America: "Public relations is a strategic communication process that builds mutually beneficial relationships between organizations and their publics."[3]

It's a bit of a mouthful, I know. But look more closely at the definition and you'll see what I like to focus on: public relations involves building good relationships.

Sometimes you need to build those relationships to help shape public knowledge of your business. Sometimes PR can help you

---

3   PRSA, "About Public Relations," accessed November 24, 2020, https://www.prsa. org/about/all-about-pr.

interpret or better understand the public attitudes toward your business and even shift that public perception. You may want to use PR to build relationships that help customers engage more with your business. You may even need PR to help protect your company's reputation.

How does it work? PR builds these relationships by promoting the public image of your business through obtaining positive coverage in publications, the news, and online. I will often describe PR in this book as earned media (as opposed to paid media).

Take another look at that illustration. In the third box, two people are discussing someone's great reputation. So, rather than the person praising himself, this image shows how good PR leads others to have a positive impression.

For your service business, generating and retaining consumer trust and confidence can be an important long-term investment. It makes sense. Consumers are much more likely to believe a news article than a paid advertisement because it's a third-party endorsement. That's the key difference. Making those connections—building those relationships—is what makes public relations unique and valuable.

THE PR DIFFERENCE

Successful businesses spend time researching other successful businesses. In this book, I'll encourage you to spend time studying your competition, to assess what they're doing well and what you can do differently. But make no mistake: it won't work for you to simply copy another company's business model. Every company's culture is slightly different. However, like an artist who is inspired by another artist's work, your business can benefit by studying successful businesses in your industry.

For instance, let's say your competitor is featured in an article in your local newspaper. You may wonder why—why was that business interviewed and not yours? If you see a competitor's owner speaking at a local chamber of commerce event, you probably wonder the same thing. How did that owner get that opportunity?

I have the answer, based on my years of experience. Your competitor has probably hired a PR agency.

Public relations experts know exactly which reporters and journalists cover your industry or the right beat, and the right PR agency can build relationships with the best of the best. Even so, it's challenging to build a trusting relationship with respected publications and outlets, and PR agencies work constantly to develop new avenues for their clients to obtain positive press. You might think it's easy to get an article in a trade or local publication, but reporters are reluctant to give coverage to one business over another, especially when they both pay for advertising.

That's why PR agencies can make a huge difference.

While it's true that advertising, marketing, and branding are valuable to your company's future, public relations builds solid relationships with business insiders and service trade groups that last. It's the connections PR agencies have in place that can help your business cut through the roadblocks to secure that earned coverage.

An effective public relations strategy can help mitigate any negative situation, but it can also help restore consumer faith and trust in your business.

PR also helps when something goes wrong.

Let's be honest. No matter how careful you are, no matter how much time you spend screening employees, triple-checking suppliers, and setting high standards for the quality of your work, things can go wrong. And often, PR is ignored until there is a crisis. You depend on your reputation in your community, and even one bad experience shared by a customer can hurt more than you might expect. An effective public relations strategy can help mitigate any negative situation, but it can also help restore consumer faith and trust in your business.

Research has proven that consumers place very little trust in advertising—a study commissioned by the American Association of Advertising Agencies shows that only 4 percent of consumers believe that advertisers and marketers practice integrity.[4] That's why consumers spend time researching your company online, rather than simply relying on ads, before choosing a home service contractor. You want that research to result in positive reviews, as well as links to articles and videos that demonstrate your expertise. If there is anything worth protecting, it is your positive reputation with your community and the homeowners you service.

We'll discuss this more later in this book, but for now, let me caution you that the last thing your business wants to do when there is a negative review or comment on social media or other media platform is respond in the wrong way. Businesses have been shuttered, CEOs have been crushed, and reputations have been ruined by negative press and social media reactions. You've undoubtedly seen plenty of stories of businesspeople who have made very bad decisions, tried to cover up their actions, and made things worse when trying to dig themselves out of a hole.

Reputation management is a function of PR that isn't always

---

4   Maureen Morrison, "No One Trusts Advertising or Media (Except Fox News)," AdAge, April 24, 2015, https://adage.com/article/media/marketers-media-trusts/298221.

given the credit it deserves, but when there is a personal or personnel crisis, a good PR strategy can be the reason a business recovers. When you think about your business, what is your most important asset? It's largely you, your reputation, and your image. Without a good reputation, businesses suffer and often fail. You have worked hard to gain respect and trust from your customers; with a crisis plan, you can be at the ready in minutes to address the situation calmly and effectively through targeted PR efforts.

For businesses suffering a natural crisis, such as a tornado, flood, wildfire, or hurricane, public relations can step in and get on it immediately, working to ease consumer and employee fears. PR will funnel the information and emergency processes to every party involved. If there is no crisis plan in place, public relations can still be effective by using existing channels to reach emergency contacts and disseminate contingency plans to the media. In a crisis, the sooner your business responds, the better it will fare in the long run, helping you not just to survive but to thrive.

You probably have dozens of competitors in your market, with more cropping up all the time. PR elevates your brand above the rest purely by leveraging visibility. However, this does not always happen through traditional PR activities. With technology changing every day and social media becoming more and more important to consumers in every industry, PR professionals like my team are constantly adapting, using new tactics to help your business reach its target audience.

I know how hard you are working to deliver great service to your customers. With the countless opportunities for promotion, it can feel impossible for a busy professional to take the time and master the technology to take advantage of these opportunities.

Let me encourage you. The techniques and strategies I'll share in the next chapters are easy for you to begin to implement. I'll also offer some expert advice on the kinds of PR you can economically manage in-house and the types of opportunities and challenges where hiring a professional may make sense.

As I mentioned earlier, good PR depends on building strong relationships. Yes, PR is evolving and changing to meet the demands of new technology and new media platforms. But personal connections are still a key way in which practitioners are promoting their clients' businesses.

For example, some home service businesses are posting videos on social media channels. Although this is a great tool to get more people to see your brand, it's how your videos are optimized that matters. Today, posting a video is not the end of the story—it should be part of an entire conversation involving marketing, advertising, branding, and PR strategies. No matter the size of your business, videos should be integrated with the overall marketing and PR plan, not just with a social media approach.

Let me explain how it works. Once a video project is in place, PR can boost the videos by pitching the series to industry or local media as part of a strategy to present your business as an industry expert. PR can also use the videos to create press releases that showcase your business as the leading expert in your home services category. Your video series, through successful PR pitching, could end up being a springboard to a home services spot on a local TV news channel.

If your business is involved in supporting or fundraising for specific charities, PR can transform your support into a newsworthy story. PR is all about storytelling, and the more impactful your story is, the better chance it has of being picked up by the media. PR takes the story from a mention on your website and transforms it into a potential feature or interview about businesses doing good and helping those less fortunate. A great example is offering your services to a struggling family through a local charity or nonprofit or providing your services free of charge to help build a home through Habitat for Humanity. You may not think it's newsworthy, but with a little boost from creative PR, there is a story to be found in even everyday business activities.

WHAT'S NEXT?

Storytelling. Building relationships. These are the keys to successful PR. No matter how technology impacts and changes how you do business, public relations is still the best way to increase the visibility your company needs to outshine the competition. PR will continue to get your story in front of your target audiences, promote you as the preferred expert, and position your business as the leader in your market.

My goal for this book is to provide you with information you can use, techniques you can try, and action steps you can follow that will give you a clear competitive advantage. I want you to succeed. I believe in the value of your home service business.

Let me show you what PR can do for you.

CHAPTER TWO

Your Strategic Analysis

When I first speak with a client, we spend a lot of time talking about strategy.

I understand—if you're like many of the great companies with whom we work, you don't have time to waste. You're focused on hiring skilled technicians, delivering superior service, and exceeding customer expectations.

You may be a bit like one of my clients, Connor.[5] Connor owns an air conditioning and heating business operating in Las Vegas—a place where they definitely need reliable air conditioning! But Connor's business is one of hundreds of heating and air companies operating in that market.

Connor came to me with some clear goals. He wanted to differentiate himself from the competition. He wanted to attract the best technicians to his business. He wanted to become the go-to air conditioning company in Las Vegas for homeowners. And he wanted

---

5   This and some other client names and locations have been changed to maintain client privacy and competitive edge.

to charge a premium price for his service.

I love a good challenge—and I had some great ideas for Connor. But first, we began with a careful strategic analysis of his positioning in the market. This is where you should always begin when planning to implement any marketing strategy.

Taking time for the kind of strategic analysis I'm recommending is an investment in your business and its long-term success. Before we can design a PR plan that makes sense for your goals, it's vital to take a clear and careful assessment of your business and to learn what it does well and where there are opportunities for growth and improvement.

So, let's begin by identifying and assessing your business's strengths, weaknesses, opportunities, and threats—what's called a SWOT analysis. You may already have performed one of these on your business, but it shouldn't be a once-and-done process. You should periodically pause and consider your company's strengths, weaknesses, opportunities, and threats to identify potential and current issues that may be impacting your business and your employees and customers.

If you want to take your business from $2 million to $5 million, or from $5 million to $10 million, you need to change some things, including how you promote your business.

Before we think about what your PR plan should incorporate, we want to identify items in each of these four categories—strengths, weaknesses, opportunities, and threats. This is a huge step that many businesses forget to do up front. A large part of your PR plan needs to come from what the SWOT analysis reveals.

Our goal will, of course, be to help you develop a strategic communications plan. If you want to take your business from $2 million to $5 million, or from $5 million to $10 million, you need to change some things, including how you promote your business.

But the first step is to take a careful look at your service business: where it started, how it has progressed (or not), where it is now, and what your goals and dreams are for the future.

This is where you need to be ruthless with yourself.

Remember the old tale about the "Emperor's New Clothes?" In it, the emperor was convinced that two new tailors would be able to craft an amazing and delicate suit for him from material so noble that only the most magnificent and intelligent of people would be able to see it. The tailors went on to say that if the person viewing the suit could not see it, he or she was ignorant and slow-witted. Of course, the emperor, being selfish and conceited, felt he must have such a suit. So when the emperor was presented with the new suit (which in fact did not exist), and the "tailors" (who were actually con men) professed that it was the most amazing suit ever, the emperor was reluctant to disagree, fearing that they would consider him ignorant. As the emperor paraded around naked in his new suit, the townspeople, servants, and nobility all pretended to admire the suit as well. They, too, did not want to be seen as ignorant. The lie spread throughout the town, like a folklore example of viral marketing. Only a small boy, who did not understand why the others were pretending to admire the invisible suit, blurted out, "But he hasn't got anything on!"

The hoax was revealed, and the emperor was confronted with the truth that even his closest advisors were unwilling to speak openly or truthfully.

There's a lesson for all of us in this folk tale. A business analysis won't work if SWOT participants aren't honest in their comments.

And the same is true of you, the business owner. As we dive deeper into the SWOT analysis, you may have to face some truths about your business that you might find unpleasant. For instance, service businesses can have an elevated sense of their market share in a particular geographic area or niche. Having performed top-of-mind recognition research and investigations for service businesses into the true market share of the business, I've discovered that many business owners often think that they have a significant market share (5–15 percent) when in fact the research and data show that they have less than a 2 percent share.

What's the lesson here? When conducting your analysis, you must be realistic. You may not have the ability to pay for an exhaustive investigation into the marketplace share of the businesses in your service area, but a good PR partner can help you perform a basic study to help you come up with a realistic figure. From that point, you can develop your strategy.

Your starting point should always be asking the right people the right questions. That's how you can begin to gather the data you'll need.

Start by asking a few key people how they would describe your business. Ask people you trust to answer honestly. Your focus group should include loyal customers, longtime employees, and peers in a best practice organization, maybe even a vendor you trust who works with similar businesses. Ask them to describe the business from its inception to today. Take note of the comments and write them down.

One of the strategies you can use as you begin to assess your business is to create a pros and cons list based on this initial feedback. Use a large easel with big tear-off sheets or a large whiteboard. As you begin to develop a strategy for your business, knowing and identifying these major areas can be crucial to reaching that next tier of success.

Not everyone is a believer in this system, and there are other similar types of business analysis tools that are available. But without spending a lot of money on research consultants and focus groups, a deep dive into your SWOTs will, at the very least, open your eyes to possibilities and risks you may not have considered before.

The information you gather for your SWOT analysis is helpful for creating a PR strategy—but its value extends even further. You can use it to create a plan or objective for a new service you're offering, and for existing services as well.

This is why your focus group is key. To make the SWOT analysis work for your service business, you will need a variety of people—not just employees or friends. I'll unpack and explain each of the four categories a bit later, but for now, just note that, for each area of the SWOT analysis, you'll want to ask diverse individuals to share their feedback. Assure them that you want their actual, uncensored thoughts. If it helps, have them do it anonymously. And be prepared for honesty.

One possibility is to create a SWOT matrix on your own, like the example below:

SWOT ANALYSIS EXAMPLE

	HELPFUL	HARMFUL
INTERNAL	STRENGTHS	WEAKNESSES
EXTERNAL	OPPORTUNITIES	THREATS

Here, you can see the different ways you can interpret SWOT data in the form of comments from participants. You might want to give them a chart like this to complete, with some basic explanations of what kind of information you're seeking.

A word of caution here. As a service business owner, you need to be aware that your SWOT in the wrong hands could be detrimental to your business. While you do want the most reliable data and comments from those you choose to include in your business assessment, be smart. Anyone filling out the SWOT questionnaire themselves should be in your presence when doing so and should hand the paper to you directly—if possible—or place it in an envelope or box only you will open.

The more feedback you get, the better. With more contributors to your SWOT analysis, you'll be able to identify consistent strengths and weaknesses. If several people notice a specific opportunity that hasn't been explored, that's a sure sign it's something to consider.

To help you translate for those filling out your SWOT form, or to explain these categories for anyone performing a SWOT analysis, here is an explanation of the terms and what they mean.

STRENGTHS OR WEAKNESSES: INTERNAL

These two categories are where you or your participants will write down the perceived strengths and weaknesses of your business from an internal point of view. An internal weakness or strength is something that you or others observe either by working there, being a customer, or through word-of-mouth from others. These are generally things that you, as the owner, could address and change, if a weakness, or build upon to achieve even greater success, if a strength.

Here are some examples of potential internal strengths your business may have:

- Skilled technicians

- Established and loyal customer base

- Good reputation built over many years

- Great culture—employees stay for many years

- Business is flat, customer base is stale

What can you take away from these strengths? If you have long-term, skilled technicians, this is a great "feel good" PR story for your local media. If you have an established customer base, you should be asking for referrals. It's a hugely successful tactic for other service businesses. Finally, collect reviews from people who have told you they value your business. Put those great comments on your website as well.

This is just a starting point. You will learn other ways to tell your target audience about your service once you have reviewed all the SWOT analysis sections and developed a business plan.

Now, let's consider some potential internal weaknesses you may uncover:

- Technicians are mostly older—no new trained techs to take over when older employees retire

- Trouble recruiting

- Nonexistent marketing of brand or business

- Technology in the office and in the field is out-of-date

- General lack of enthusiasm, no momentum

This is a much bleaker picture, but remember that you're not looking for compliments or praise. You want honesty so you can respond strategically. Knowing that your business has these perceived internal weaknesses, you could create a plan that would address them strategically and in a targeted way, based upon the overall plan developed from your SWOT.

Overcoming weaknesses is a process to be considered carefully and by examining all four of the SWOT analysis sections as a whole. Once you review your opportunities and threats, you'll have a better idea of which of these weaknesses needs attention now, which needs to be addressed soon, and which can be addressed later.

OPPORTUNITIES AND THREATS: EXTERNAL

External opportunities and threats are factors that affect your business that are out of your direct control. For instance, the economy, political climate, geography, weather, business regulations, and new laws are things you, as an individual business owner, cannot control. Some of these external factors can be seen as opportunities and some can be seen as threats. It's up to you to carefully examine the business climate for your service area and determine which factors threaten your success and which present opportunities, and how you want to look at them.

Some potential external threats your SWOT analysis may reveal:

- There are several other quality home service businesses or franchise brands in the market

- A sizable portion of homes in the market are less than ten years old

- Competitors are spending a lot of marketing dollars

- Government regulation making it more expensive to do business

- Large home improvement stores increasing contractor competition

- Newer service businesses encroaching with flashy trucks and equipment

- Technology is leaving your business behind

Threats can often be turned around, and, with a little ingenuity, many can become opportunities. In the list above, competition is listed as a threat. While it's true that more competition can be perceived as a threat, when your business is a known entity with a solid customer base and a good reputation, you can use this new competition as an opportunity to counter their "new kid on the block" marketing theme by spreading the word about your well-respected and well-known brand. Big-box home improvement stores can be a threat to some businesses; you can change your messaging to communicate why the homeowner should choose your reputable company.

Another threat is lack of technology. This is a big problem with many existing service businesses. Investing in updating your technology should not be overlooked. Some software may even help identify ways that your company is losing money or help your technicians increase their average ticket.

Potential external opportunities:

- Adding a new service line

- Rebranding your company name

- Government incentives and rebates for equipment upgrades

- Younger technicians looking for stable work in the area

- Competing local papers offering discounts on digital and print advertising

All the above offer great potential for expanding or increasing your company's revenue. With loan regulations making small business loans an option, you can take advantage of these new opportunities to update equipment and add new technology to make your business more efficient. Along with improved efficiencies, new technology can be a selling point to existing customers and attract new customers as well. If the longtime technicians are very skilled, but they're looking to retire sometime soon, hiring younger "green" technicians to be mentored who may have different skill sets is a great opportunity. An established business can be more attractive to younger technicians looking for stability.

> **Along with improved efficiencies, new technology can be a selling point to existing customers and attract new customers as well.**

Along with adding new technology, updating an existing website can be extremely helpful. When local papers compete for your advertising dollars, it's a win for businesses. If print ads come with digital components, take advantage of them. But make sure your own website has a great call-to-action page where digital ads send potential customers. Without a call-to-action page on your website, digital advertising will have less impact on your ability to acquire new customers through online platforms—and that is where you have the greatest potential to grab new clients. We'll talk more about strategies for effective website development later in this book.

Finally, identify the SWOT areas that are harmful or helpful to round out your overall view of the business. Once you have as many comments as you feel you need to complete your analysis in all areas of the SWOT diagram, then it's time to create your business or action plan.

FROM ANALYSIS TO ACTION

A SWOT analysis is basically a first step in a strategic business plan. Your next steps depend on your ability to take action on the items identified as the most important to the success of your business. Look at the strengths and opportunities, and choose the top five that can be used to the greatest advantage. Then look at the weaknesses and threats, and determine the most critical areas to address. Choose the top five areas that need to be taken care of as soon as possible.

Once you have your SWOT Top 10 list, you can devise a plan. There are other SWOT follow-up plans on the internet, and it may be helpful to look at other completed SWOT projects through a Google search. Through this research, you may even find other areas that you missed or weren't aware of that you can add to your own analysis. But remember that adding too many options to your plan can slow you down on your path to becoming more successful.

Based on the Top 10 list you created, your action plan should include the following bullets:

- Designate specific employees to follow up on specific items from the SWOT Top 10 list.

- Create a timeline for investigation, research, and development so that employees have the ability to become knowledgeable about their assignment.

- Schedule follow-up meetings to share and learn findings after the research and investigation phase.

- During follow-up meetings, you may learn of unknown factors that can affect the action plan, and you may need to adapt and revise the Top 10 list as you go.

- Once all the items on the list have been vetted and investigated, costs and expenses have been collected, and the realistic options available to you and your business are taken together as a whole, that is when you create your strategic action plan.

This is a lot harder than you think, but the payoff is that you will have a clear understanding of your market, your strengths, your weaknesses, your opportunities, and your threats. And that is when the fun begins—you can use your knowledge to set new goals and develop a PR strategy.

Remember, your competition is likely not doing a SWOT analysis—or any analysis. So you already have an advantage. In the next chapter, we'll dig deeper into ways you can infiltrate your competition—figuratively—to gain insight and use it to your advantage.

CHAPTER THREE

Know Your Competition

Six Rivers Plumbing is experiencing a challenge common to many in the trades: recruiting skilled technicians. Keeping them is even more challenging.

The owner of Six Rivers discovered that many of his best technicians were leaving his business after only a year or two and going to work for one of his biggest competitors. He came to me, expressing his frustration and asking for help.

My answer surprised him—I told him to solve the mystery first. Why were his technicians leaving? What was his competitor offering, and why was it so attractive?

Sometimes good PR planning depends upon some basic detective work. You need to know what your competitors are doing well—and what they aren't—to identify opportunities and understand challenges.

I'm sure that you've heard the expression "imitation is the sincerest form of flattery." I suggest a different approach. Watch your competition, or even businesses outside your industry, and rather than imitate directly, adapt their successful strategies to your own business.

Some of the best home service businesses I know have visited Disney, Zappos, Nordstrom, and other successful companies outside the industry to learn what they are doing to experience strategic growth.

See what these companies do right and what they do wrong; go to their workshops or schedule a tour of their headquarters. Watch their ads in print, on social media, and on Google searches. Listen to see if they have ads on the radio. Read the newspapers and trade journals for your service business regularly to see which company is getting press and media coverage.

Now, write down what you want *your* business to achieve.

DO YOUR RESEARCH

If you search online for the keywords you want to be known for, you will naturally see your competitors come up in Google search results. This is an important part of your research.

First, you will want to look at your competitors' websites. Begin by thinking like a potential customer. If your service business is mainly residential plumbing, type the words you think potential customers will most likely type into the search engine search bar, and include your specific city or geographical market. This will show businesses like yours in the area near you. If you service Denver and you type in the search bar "plumbing repair," you'll get thousands of results. Don't worry about all of them. Focus only on the first page. The first page of the results is where you want your business to appear. If it doesn't, you have some work to do.

Second, check out which businesses show up on the first page organically. These are the listings that appear *under* the "sponsored ads." The difference is that paid ads through Google's AdWords program appear at the top of the search results page. These ads look very much like an organic search result, except there is a little box to the left of the URL line of the ad (usually the second or third line under the search result headline) that says "Ad." The organic listings do not have the word "Ad" next to the URL.

How businesses show up on the first page organically is based on a number of factors. Some of these include how long the website has been active, how many visitors go to the site, how many links go to other verified websites, whether the website is mentioned on other sites, if the site appears in news stories, if there is new content added to the site regularly on a blog, how many positive reviews there are, how active the brand is on social media pages that link to the site, and many other factors. You could make a case that brands appearing organically on the first page are doing pretty well with their public relations.

Through AdWords, or paid advertising, your business can appear on the first page for certain search terms or keywords depending on your budget, which keywords or phrases you want to target, and what audiences you want to reach, but we will come back to paid ads later in this chapter.

The third thing that you'll want to pay attention to when researching competitor websites is this: What are those businesses doing that you are not, aside from paid ads? You want to investigate the top websites of your competitors in the organic results. Spend some time going to each page of your competitors' websites. Take on the persona of a homeowner, and try to think objectively as you navigate the website. Jot down the pros and cons of each website. The list could look like this:

Joey's Plumbing Services
Pros
- Very attractive graphically

- Loads very quickly, no lag time

- Call to action is visible on home page

- Phone number and email links are clickable from a mobile device

- Brand logo is recognizable and simple

Cons

- Very cluttered home page

- Website content is too long, wordy

- Can't find what I am looking for, difficult navigation

- Website requires excessive scrolling

- Images look very old or grainy

Do this for every major competitor you have. Don't waste a lot of time on competitors who don't do better than you do on search engine results, but pay close attention to the ones who have favorable positions or rankings on Google, Yahoo, Bing, or other search engines.

Finally, when you perform a search using keywords or phrases that fit your business, see if a map appears on the first page of the search results. A map with businesses pinpointed in red that correspond to a listing below the map is another way Google encourages businesses to use its products. The only way to show up on that map is to have a Google My Business page. Which businesses show up on Google Maps' first three to five listings can sometimes be more important to a potential customer than the organic results or paid ads. Typically, a customer will see the top three to five listings on the map and click on the links provided by the Google map.

How your business appears on the map is a well-kept secret, and Google is in no hurry to explain its algorithms and how they work.

But people who do this for a living can extrapolate certain common denominators that appear to help with placement on the maps:

- The number of real reviews on Google My Business

- Having an active Google My Business page

- Making sure all the information on your business page matches your website and other online pages

- Having a well-ranked and updated website

You can find out how to create a Google My Business page on Google's Help pages or through an internet search, but there are many nuances to creating a page that gets noticed, is done right, and will help your business show up on Google Maps. I'll share my recommendations for your website later in this book.

Once you have reviewed and written down your competition's website pros and cons, decide which aspects you might want to change on your own website. I hope that you've performed the SWOT analysis I recommended in chapter two; this is an opportunity to use those SWOT

An effective and well-executed public relations plan will help with all your company's efforts to be more visible online, no matter what the platform.

analysis results to help revise your website and make it into an effective marketing tool.

But never underestimate the power of public relations to make all your efforts worthwhile. An effective and well-executed public relations plan will help with all your company's efforts to be more visible online, no matter what the platform: website, social, news sites, YouTube, Google Maps, and more.

REVIEW YOUR COMPETITION'S SOCIAL PLATFORMS

It's still a Facebook, Instagram, Twitter, and YouTube world for most service businesses. Technically, these forms of promotion are free. This means you don't pay to play. That's part of the reason why many social media providers are so interested in monetizing their platforms. You can buy ads on most social media platforms and that is where they make a lot of money. But while some businesses may dabble in many social media platforms, the main players for service businesses remain Facebook, Instagram, Twitter, and YouTube.

What's great about these platforms is that they provide a way to gauge how well your public relations efforts are doing. In the past, PR agencies weren't quick to adapt to social media, and lagged behind other marketers and marketing businesses. Today, PR that doesn't include social media is a rarity. And that's a good thing.

So your next step, as a service business wanting to improve its competitive edge, is to research your competitors' social media pages. There are many ways to do this, but the most obvious is to go to their pages and see what they are posting. Take the competitors you found from your website research and go to their websites again, but this time with your focus firmly on their social media accounts.

Start with the home page. See where the social media icons are located, and click on each one to get to their social media pages. You won't have time to read each post, but what you want to notice first is how their pages are set up. Are they done professionally? Does the company actually own the rights to the images they are using? Are the posts grammatically correct? Do they look like an amateur wrote them? If so, that might actually be the case, and while it may seem financially attractive to have one of your call takers or someone else with some extra time on their hands take on the additional responsibility for social media, this can and does backfire. Make sure you have someone with a strong business acumen in charge of your online reputation.

Next, after you have observed the Facebook, Instagram, Twitter, and YouTube pages of your competitors, do a little deeper analysis. See how your company's social media pages compare to theirs. What do you like about their pages that you don't like about yours? What captures your interest or makes you want to go back to their pages? Think about what you want people to learn when they go to your pages. Have your competitors accomplished what you want for your business on their social pages?

In addition to researching your top competitors' social media, look at the social pages of nationally known service businesses. These businesses are probably using PR professionals and marketing companies to manage their social pages. Do the same analysis on these well-known brands' social pages. What do you like about them? What makes these pages different from your pages or those of your local competitors?

It's time for some strategic analysis. What can you take from your research and start doing on your own pages?

Begin with one platform and write down the things you like about each company's page. If you start with Facebook, do a basic inventory to help you fine-tune what you like and don't like about other service business Facebook pages.

Some possibilities to consider as you assemble your Facebook main page likes:

- New posts every day/week

- Attractive and branded well

- Lots of good photos

- Posts are not all about selling (I recommend 80 percent informative and educational posts, 20 percent promotional)

- People react positively to posts or make lots of comments

- The business responds to the comments quickly

- Negative issues are resolved off-line—not on the social page

These are the very visible aspects of a Facebook page. For instance, Facebook allows users to change out the main page photo. Some businesses change it out every week. Others keep the main photo the same so customers do not become confused and think they are on a different Facebook page. It's up to you.

Now perform the same careful assessment for Facebook main page dislikes for each competitor. What have you learned? Make sure to eliminate things you don't like from your page.

One thing to keep in mind when working with social media: it's instant. And by that, I mean that it can give you instant gratification or it can send your business into a rabbit hole from which you or your business may struggle to recover if you are not careful. That's another reason why a seasoned communications pro is a better choice to manage your company's social media. Make sure the person you use has some relevant experience managing a professional business social media account.

We have not touched on Instagram, Twitter, and YouTube yet, but the same research techniques used for Facebook can also be used to review your competitors' YouTube channels and Twitter and Instagram feeds. Having a strong presence on Instagram can help you create a savvy and current brand while showing your company's personality, and Twitter is key for search engine optimization, but none of the social media platforms should be taken lightly. Be very intentional with all your social media posts, whether videos or text or images. These platforms have a very long memory, and while posts can get lost in the pure volume of other posts, a poor choice of words, an image that others can take the wrong way, or a typo that looks like something else could create trouble.

Remember that much of your business now and in the future will be ever more dependent on your online presence (or nonpresence).

After doing this kind of strategic social media research, you will be much savvier about what kind of social media pages you want for your business. After all, it's your business. It deserves careful analysis for protection and promotion.

WHAT ABOUT TRADITIONAL FORMS OF PROMOTION?

Earlier in this book, I mentioned the term *earned media*. This is what every businessperson covets. Free publicity. But how do you get earned media coverage in newspapers, TV, radio, trade journals, and other industry publications? It's not easy.

As part of your competitive analysis, you'll undoubtedly see some of your competitors quoted, interviewed, or popping up as an expert in an article or on TV. Pay attention to what they're saying and where they're appearing.

Now, we can consider what this means for your own PR strategy. Let's start with how to get free attention from media. There are many routes you can take to try and get media to pay attention to your business and to call you for a quote when they are covering a story about your industry. If you want reporters, writers, and TV news stations to cover you or your business, you have to give them something in return.

As a former contributing journalist myself, I have a great perspective on what media need from businesses to get their job done. It's pretty simple:

1. Tell the truth.

2. Be available for an interview or quote when they call.

3. Have a point of view you can talk about easily.

4. Be a subject matter expert.

5. Be comfortable speaking on camera or to reporters.

It's not as easy as 1, 2, 3, 4, and 5. There is research involved here as well.

I'll share my strategies for successful media interviews and appearances later in this book, but for now, let me give you a few key recommendations. Become a reader. Read other industry or company blogs, read their articles, and check out trade journals where similar businesses are quoted. Become familiar with the journalists and reporters who cover your industry in a variety of publications and on TV or radio station websites. Send them a note praising their recent story about your industry, follow them on Facebook and LinkedIn, and comment once in a while on their posts. Retweet their tweets that are relevant to your business on Twitter. Like their Facebook posts and their pages.

A word of warning here: Be careful not to appear as if you are stalking them. It's a fine line; knowing how much is too much is important when working with media.

It takes time to cultivate relationships with the media, but once you do, they will come to depend on you for a quick soundbite, a quote, or an on-air interview. Being the subject matter expert in your area is a moving target, so you must always be on the alert for a good story, and when you pitch it to your media contacts, hopefully they will bite.

PAID ADS AND OTHER PROMOTIONAL MATERIALS

What about print ads, radio ads, TV ads, and other traditional marketing and PR efforts? Are you spotting your competitors there? Again, think strategically about what they are doing—and why. What insights can you gain from this research, and how will it impact your own planning?

Print ads are often somewhat of a luxury, because the cost is very high for the perceived return on investment. Businesses pay dearly for ads, but there can sometimes be very little proof that a print, radio, or TV ad worked.

These ads can be tracked via codes on incentives or unique phone numbers or URLs. But more commonly, paid ad successes are hard to track. For this reason, many businesses use print ads in newspapers and magazines as branding ads. Rather than expecting to get a certain number of calls from an advertisement, more businesses are using ads as a way to keep their brand top of mind with consumers.

There is nothing wrong with this type of ad campaign. But if you are short on budget dollars for branding-type ads, there are other ways to promote your business via paid ads that are easier to track and may even work better than your current advertising mix.

Let's consider digital ads. You included these in your analysis of your competitors, but now I want to discuss how they can impact your PR goals. Online ads could be AdWords text ads, image ads, ads that link to your website or a specific landing page, banner ads that appear on a publication website on the top or bottom or the side of website pages, and any number of other paid ads that appear on other websites. Other ways to promote your business are available on media websites and social media platforms.

Most, if not all, of these advertisement options allow you, the business owner, to track your ad. This can be done in a number of ways and depends on the platform, but in general, you should be able to see, through a dashboard, how well your ad is doing at any moment in time. AdWords by Google has a very detailed dashboard that can be extremely time-consuming to try to learn on your own, so you may want to partner with a specialist digital agency who will work with you not only to set up your AdWords account, but also to create ads and track them.

Things that you can track include:

- Where people who clicked on your ads come from

- What devices people were on when they clicked on your ad

- Exactly how many people clicked on your ad in a specific time frame (you can set up the specifics of how you want to track your ads)

- What time of day was the most popular time for ad viewership

- What it costs you per ad click and per day (you can also set a budget)

- Which keywords or terms got the highest clicks

That's only the beginning. We could devote a whole chapter to AdWords and still not touch on every aspect of this popular but complicated platform. AdWords is not for the casual browser. It is an effective way to track ads so users can really see where their money is going. One thing it allows users to do that is great: you can change your ads quickly. You can alter, revise, tweak, edit, or even delete your ads in seconds.

What makes it even better is the ability to look at each ad's performance over time so that you can target your ad to reach a very specific audience. Through trial and error, you can use AdWords to help you determine the right keywords that your target audience responds to, thus making your advertising more effective and cost-efficient.

I realize that this kind of research takes time to do well. But the information you'll uncover is very valuable.

It will equip you to create more targeted ways to promote your business. It will give you insight into how you can more effectively establish your name and your brand.

And it just may help you solve the mystery of how to respond to a competitor's challenge.

NEXT LEVEL

NOW

CHAPTER FOUR

Designing Your PR Strategy

"I want to create 99 millionaires."

It's not unusual for my clients to want to become millionaires, but when a client says that his goal is to make other business owners millionaires—99 of them—well, I definitely was intrigued.

What this client—we'll call him Jack—was proposing was to identify other home service businesses in his industry—businesses that were struggling, that had owners who were passionate and skilled technical experts but had plateaued. They had reached a certain level and couldn't seem to grow the business beyond that.

Jack had experienced great success in his industry; he was a millionaire many times over. And he wanted to share his expertise with others in his industry. He wanted to create 99 millionaires by buying those businesses, keeping the owners on as general managers, and helping them to build their companies and their wealth. He wanted us to help develop a PR strategy to promote this campaign nationally—to let businesses know that, if they wanted Jack's help, if they wanted to be acquired, if they wanted to become one of his 99 millionaires, they should contact him.

Not every client has a goal like this one. But no matter your business, no matter your goal, a PR strategy can help you reach the next level.

So now it's time to begin to create that strategy. You've created a business plan. You've analyzed your company's performance in the industry, and you have a very good handle on how your business needs to change and adapt. You are aware of your competitors and their strengths and weaknesses. You know what needs to be done, and you're busy working on the business and ready to do what it takes to grow.

Now you need an effective public relations strategy. Good PR makes you and your brand visible to the right people and positions you as an expert so you're the one people call when they need service. Good PR helps create a positive online presence and reputation so when people look up your reviews—and they will—they'll trust you and your business. And good PR funnels potential customers to your website, where visitors will follow a sales path to take action. That's the road to generating more sales and less stress.

THE TRUTH ABOUT PUBLIC RELATIONS

We've talked about what PR is—and what it isn't—earlier in this book. Remember, PR involves building successful relationships. But let's dive a bit deeper here to really understand the truth about PR.

If you look up public relations online, Google gives this definition: "The professional maintenance of a favorable public image by a company or other organization or a famous person." This to me, as a public relations agency business owner and a PR expert, is very similar to how I envision what a PR professional should aim to do. We help foster positive impressions about you.

There are some other definitions that are worth reading:

Merriam-Webster says: "Public relations is the business of inducing the public to have understanding for and goodwill toward a person, firm, or institution."

Dictionary.com's definition: "Public relations is the actions of a corporation, store, government, individual, etc., in promoting goodwill between itself and the public, the community, employees, consumers, etc."

There's nothing negative in any of those definitions. Yet people sometimes talk about PR as if it's a questionable activity or something that is really all about spin rather than strategically putting out positive messaging.

It's true that sometimes PR practitioners can send messaging out into the world that's a little shady. I'm sure that you can think of a few examples. The thing to remember is that if you fudge anything, you'll be found out at some point. And if that happens,

Reputation is everything in both business-to-business and business-to-consumer relationships. Trying to put spin on something that could backfire is never your best strategy.

it's nearly impossible to recover your reputation. Reputation is everything in both business-to-business and business-to-consumer relationships. Trying to put spin on something that could backfire is never your best strategy.

PR practitioners know this, and it is a standard among ethical professionals to be transparent in any campaign. The problem arises when people who are not trained in public relations try to do the job, only to find out there is a lot more to PR than writing press releases.

YOUR NEXT STEPS IN A GOOD PR PLAN

I talk about PR strategy for a reason. PR is a multifaceted and well-organized plan of action focusing on making your business or product visible to its target audience with the goal of encouraging that audience to take action.

You have done a SWOT analysis and studied your competition. You have a good basis now to take all this information and create a PR plan to help your service business grow and prosper, enabling you to make more money, work less, and purchase that new truck or hire more service experts.

PR professionals are adept at taking all this information and creating an overall plan that will hit all the most important targets. The strategies may differ from business to business, but the plan must include action items—real activities that you, your employees, or a PR agency working on your behalf will need to make happen.

You may ultimately decide to hire a PR expert—we'll discuss how to identify when this makes sense later in the book. But the good news is that there are some basic strategies you can put in place today, right now, to help leverage the knowledge you've gathered into a plan to promote your business and create that goodwill that the definitions described.

The first step? Gather the information you collected and map out your comprehensive PR plan. This can be done in a variety of ways, but it is good to have a whiteboard or a bare wall where you can put large sticky notes before starting a project like this. In large PR agencies, there are rooms that are used to brainstorm, much like writers' rooms for TV sitcoms or late-night shows. The rooms are where the creatives sit and write ideas on large blackboards, giant Post-its, or flip boards. In my agency, we have an entire whiteboard wall in one of our brainstorming and strategy rooms.

Begin by creating columns that list all the key things you've discovered through your competitive research and SWOT analysis. This list should include the following:

- Your strengths

- Your weaknesses

- Your competition's strengths

- Your competition's weaknesses

- Media coverage (good and bad)

- Advertising (success or failures)

- Your social media presence (what is working and what isn't)

Next, use the information from your SWOT analysis and competitive research and place each key item you've identified under the correct category.

It's easy to get overwhelmed by the number of items you're listing. But this is just an initial starting point. Your ultimate plan will reflect your budget, and your staffing and time availability. You may not be able to accomplish everything on the plan immediately. The beauty of a PR plan, however, is that it's not, and should not be, a static thing. It's always changing, and you need to adapt and change as your needs change.

Start with strengths at the top of the list, and review all the items that appear in that category. Your goal, as you develop your PR plan, is to create a list of action items. Action items are the things that need to happen to enhance existing strengths. Maybe your website does very well on organic searches. That's a great thing. You can keep it going by doing more of what makes it so popular. The goal is to list three actions that will make those strengths even better. Another strength could be your current technicians. If you get positive comments from customers about the technicians, one of the actions could be to place those testimonials on your website. Good PR is all about visibility, positive reinforcement, and public awareness, and PR professionals are adept at homing in on which actions are the most visible.

Under weaknesses, you want to build a list of actions that can be done to turn a weakness into a strength. If a weakness is that the public is not aware of your business, think of what your competition is doing that you aren't. Do they have a really great brand and colorful trucks with impactful graphics and messaging? What would be an effective way to combat that? Researching specialist branding agencies would be a first line of approach. If a weakness is a low conversion rate from website inquiries to phone calls, maybe an action would include training call takers and CSRs to make outbound calls. If they are not properly trained and incentivized, you won't have great conversion rates. These are just examples of how to take a weakness and create an action plan to turn the weakness around. The advantage of partnering with a PR agency specializing in the home service industry is that these actions are easily accomplished and the know-how is already there.

Your competitor's strengths and weaknesses are another opportunity to enhance your public relations plan. Under competitor strengths, take their lead and list ways your business can use their successes to your advantage. Rather than just copying their PR activities, you'll want to revise and tweak them to fit your business. If your competitors are doing a lot of TV appearances, you may want to find out from those TV stations how you can achieve similar results. Or better yet, contact the TV station's competitor in the market and find out if they have a program to help businesses get more attention on a budget. Some TV stations have sales staff who are able to give free advice and counseling to businesses. Some also offer creation and production of a TV spot if you commit to a specific rotation or time spot, etc. This may be one area where you'll want to consider working with a professional PR agency. They do have a distinct advantage over a single business in that having an already established media funnel makes the process simple, and their negotiation skills for earned rather than paid media may be more advanced.

Under your competitor's weaknesses, list opportunities to take advantage of those weaknesses. What if your competitor has been around for forty years or more and has dated marketing materials? You can use their weaknesses to help your business. Position your company as *the* company that can save clients more time and money by doing things right the first time. You may want to highlight the fact that your service experts use field technology for diagnoses and are highly skilled in new installs. Keep a vigilant eye on competitor activities, as they are probably watching you too.

When it comes to media coverage, professionals definitely have the advantage in this aspect of PR. It's a very hard nut to crack. Media have a directive to only cover what is news, and they do not want to be accused of favoring one business over another in the eyes of their audience. Especially in today's news environment, favoring any business or entity over another is taken very seriously. How do the PR professionals do it? Very slowly and studiously, with a lot of research, and by making the life of a reporter or news station easier. Press releases are just the tip of the iceberg when attempting to get earned media coverage. Knowing whom to contact, when to contact them, and with what kind of pitch is a big part of the work PR agencies do to get coverage.

For small businesses, the best strategy is to watch, listen, and read diligently to see who in your local area covers stories that relate to your business. Research your trade group publications to see who covers what. Some publications have editorial calendars, and if you study those, you can target your news releases to coincide with the theme of particular journals or magazines in your industry.

Keep a list of media contacts, and send them genuine news about your business, and you will forge relationships that will help you grow your business over time. Plan to keep media aware of your successes, your charitable work, your staff promotions, new equipment purchases, and more. But make sure to thank them any time you get coverage, and always let them know you are available for interviews and comments. Being available is extremely important, as news happens without warning and your expert opinion could be just what a reporter needs to help them with a story. We'll talk more about presenting a professional media appearance later in this book—don't try to wing it!

If you do get negative coverage, make it your mission to address it with the reporter in a nice and calm manner. Never lose your temper with media. The same careful approach is true for social media: never hurl out tweets and Facebook posts that you will regret later. Your reputation is important, and being courteous will go a long way. Let the reporter know there are two sides to each story and that you are happy to clarify the events. If you were in the wrong, the best course of action is to admit it, apologize, make it right, and move on. Never place blame on the media if you want to have a positive relationship. PR agencies are regularly called in to handle a business crisis, and for good reason. A true crisis that is not handled carefully can literally end a business.

Your PR plan may also include communications in your advertising. Under the advertising category, examine your past advertising, what worked and what didn't, and compare your ads to those of your competitors. Then, create an action plan under this category as well.

While PR is not the same as advertising, many PR agencies help clients create impactful ads, and often a PR and communications plan includes advertising as a part of the overall strategy. Your ads may also solidify messaging that you are trying to promote through other PR activities. One of the best things you can do for your business is to manage your ads' success through analysis after the fact. In your ads, place codes for potential customers to use when calling your business. The codes will help you quantify the ad's success. But that won't tell the whole picture.

Trying to see if an ad is successful is not yet a science. Print ads are notoriously hard to analyze. A potential customer may see a print ad several times, and then go to the advertiser's website to learn more. When they call, they may say they researched your business on the internet, without even mentioning they saw your ad three times in the local paper.

So, when creating action items under advertising, keep all these things in mind. You'll be better able to find out the effectiveness of online ads like banner ads and AdWords ads through the analytics tools available through websites or Google Analytics. Analytics programs are complex tools that can take a lot of time and effort to master, and even then, the platforms update and change frequently.

Finally, list what you are doing right and wrong with your social media, and note the good and bad about your competitor's platforms. You then can create an action plan from the observations you have made.

I've talked about social media, but it's worth noting here that if you don't have social media accounts for your business, this is your chance to take the leap and join the rest of the world. Social media is no longer a flash in the pan that will lose its appeal over time. It can be a very effective part of an overall communications plan. I would even venture to say that if you do not participate in social media, your business is doing itself an injustice.

PR and social media go hand in hand to help create an effective image-building process. In addition, with effective social media, you can improve your Google ranking, increase your company's social imprint, and create a positive impression online.

The caveat is that you must be active on your social platforms. We'll talk more about social media strategy later, but for now, let's review a few simple steps for your plan. If you set up a Facebook account for your business, make sure you post to it regularly. Ask employees, customers, or clients to like and follow your business page. The general rule of thumb is to post items of interest to your audience 80 percent of the time and promote your own products or services 20 percent of the time. The idea is that you want to show your audience that you are not just trying to sell them something and that you have a genuine interest in educating them and sharing good content with them. That's a better way to increase your audience and get more likes than if your page is all about promotion.

When your brainstorming is complete, when you have action items for each category and have identified which items are critical, you're ready to write a formal plan of action. You may not be able to do all those things, but highlight the most important one in each category and make it a priority to do it.

As a guideline, think of your strategic PR plan as having buckets. Each bucket is an area of PR that you need to address to garner more positive attention for your business, and as a result, more clients and customers.

CHAPTER FIVE

Is Your Social Media an Afterthought?

When you are operating a successful business, your time is precious. Making sure that your Facebook page or Instagram stories are regularly updated may not be a top priority. Maybe someone in your office is responsible for finding funny pictures and posting them to your social media account when they have extra time.

Would it surprise you to learn that having inexperienced people handle social media has actually been the death knell for some companies? This is one of the most important things you do, simply because that's where your business can have direct communication with potential customers. If you regularly write and share blogs that help your readers and offer tips and solutions, people are more likely to engage with you and your page. However, it's important to be aware that social media needs constant monitoring and nurturing. And, even more importantly, social media pages often influence journalists. When your news release or pitch comes across their desk, if they've never heard of your company, they're going to do a quick Google search. What they find can make or break their decision to do a positive story about your company. Managing social media is best done carefully and strategically.

Part of that strategic thinking involves deciding how social media can help you speak to existing customers and reach potential customers. One key element of this is knowing which social media platforms those customers use. Facebook, Twitter, and Instagram all have different users who engage with these platforms for different reasons and with different goals.

Another element of this strategic thinking is identifying how to communicate with those customers. Clever messages, funny pictures, and informative videos all can be used effectively—but one may be more appropriate for your customer and for your brand's unique style of communication than the others.

One of my clients—a home service business owner based in Virginia Beach—is very comfortable talking on camera. Whenever there is a storm or hurricane in the weather forecast, he uses that as an opportunity to speak directly to his customers. He doesn't need expensive video equipment; he just uses his smartphone's camera to share a message about the weather and how it may impact their home. He shoots a thirty-second or sixty-second selfie-style video with some tips and helpful information. He has a friendly face and a great personality that comes across in every video. People just love him!

These kinds of videos are a great way to connect with both loyal customers and prospective customers on social media. I encourage you to consider whether this is a strategy that makes sense for your business. I'll discuss more about media appearances and share some tips for effective communication when you're on camera later in this book. For now, let me just add that there is great value in a friendly, knowledgeable technician or owner speaking directly to customers—not in a scripted way, not as if they are delivering an advertisement, but instead as if they are sharing information designed to keep people safe and comfortable in their homes. A real person speaking to real people.

If your company uses social media, that's a great start. But as I noted earlier, it's more about *how* you use it than *if* you use it. Think about your business whenever you post something on social media. What are you trying to say? Who are you saying it to? What are you hoping to achieve with your posts? These are critical questions to ask whenever you choose to share something on your social media channels.

In your personal life, you can choose to share informal photos with friends, respond casually to messages, comment on posts, or quickly update your status. But your professional social media activities need to be managed very differently. Posts and updates should never be casual or off the cuff. You always want to be thoughtful, considering the three questions I noted earlier: What is my message? Who will see it? What do I want to accomplish?

Social media posts sometimes have a way of getting out into the mainstream news channels either by accident or by intentional means. They can also be quoted as company statements in a crisis, as we have seen over and over again on Twitter and Facebook. Social posts by celebrities, sports figures, and even ordinary people or businesses can and do backfire. If you think a certain post might offend someone, it probably will, and the best policy is not to post it, because it could hurt your business.

> **If you think a certain post might offend someone, it probably will, and the best policy is not to post it, because it could hurt your business.**

The other thing to remember is this: your online posts never die. Even after posts have been removed, a record of them may still exist.

Those who saw them could have easily taken a screenshot. They may have been forwarded, copied, or duplicated. You should always post with the understanding that it will live on in perpetuity.

It's important to remember that many of your customers will find your business after an online search. That means that they will see not only your website but also your social media platforms. It's always a good policy to keep a very careful eye on what your social media pages are saying, because whatever is being put out there is likely to be seen, regardless of how many likes or followers you have. You might be surprised to know that your posts can be shared, and if your security settings allow your posts to be seen by the public, many more people than you think could see your posts. Most of the time, that is a good thing. But remember that news is news, whether it is good or bad, and media attention can be positive or negative.

Another thing to keep in mind is that news shared on social media travels fast. More and more people are getting their news online or on mobile devices than ever before. The trend is continuing, with no sign of letting up.

The importance of online and digital channels in providing news was highlighted in a 2019 Pew Research Study. The results may surprise you: 34 percent of Americans indicated that they preferred to get their news online, compared with 28 percent in 2016.[6] It's especially important to consider the statistics for *local* news, since this may have the greatest impact on your home service business. Roughly four in ten Americans say that they prefer to get their local news via online channels—almost equal to the number that prefer accessing local news via TV. And an astonishing 77 percent say that the internet

---

6   A. W. Geiger, "Key findings about the online news landscape in America,"
    Pew Research Center, September 11, 2019, https://www.pewresearch.org/
    fact-tank/2019/09/11/key-findings-about-the-online-news-landscape-in-america/.

is important in how they get local news.

What does this have to do with social media and public relations? What these statistics show is that people are spending more and more time online and less time reading traditional print materials for their news—and traditional print media outlets are increasingly relying on their online news pages. As more people spend more time online, the businesses that are active and responsive on social media will be able to communicate with their audiences more directly and interactively than is possible with traditional print.

I know that some will argue that magazines and niche publications are great places to promote a business or product. And that may be true in some cases, say for B2B businesses, but for the majority of B2C home service businesses, getting the word out via online channels and media outlets with an online presence is where business is heading. You want to be where your customers are, using platforms that speak to them in the most effective ways.

That's why we spend time working with clients to create a social media strategy. PR's involvement in social media is a no-brainer. If two concepts were ever meant to live in harmony, it is social media and PR. As a public relations professional, I want to make sure that your business or product is viewed by its target audience in the very best possible light. That means focusing not just on your product or service, but on your reputation. I know that we play a key role as a reputation manager. It's not just a matter of maintaining a client's existing reputation; we also want to cultivate and nurture a good reputation for them. This can help them mitigate crises, in part by developing a reputation for being both responsive and transparent.

Social media has become one of the most visible platforms any business has today, aside from its website. That's why I'm encouraging you to think strategically about how to best use social media to promote your brand, get attention from your target audience, and obtain coverage from the media.

You can see that social media management is a big job and not something that should be tackled by anyone in the office with a few extra hours a week or a team member with a marketing degree but no relevant experience. Public relations firms like mine have stepped into the social media sphere in large part to supply both strategic marketing and reputation-enhancing communications. We know that businesses like yours need someone to take charge of how your business is being viewed and managed online, because as Facebook and Twitter and other platforms have matured, so has the need for more sophisticated management of those channels.

No longer can your business depend on the posting of an image of a service truck, an employee's birthday party, or your office Labrador (cute though she may be) to garner trust and loyalty from your customers. Social media can give your business a big boost, or it can be a dud; either of these may have a real impact on your business's success or failure.

TIPS FOR TAKING CHARGE OF YOUR SOCIAL MEDIA

As platforms like Facebook, Twitter, and Instagram have grown and become more complex, getting the most out of them for businesses has itself become a business.

Try this experiment: type "social media marketing for business" into a search engine like Google. You will likely get similar search results to mine: more than two million results. This proves that social media marketing is a very big business. There are plenty of places to find advice, plenty of claims about return on investment and increasing business.

So what are the things that are going to get your business attention and more customers on social media channels? Let me share a few tips that I share with my clients—strategies that have proven to be successful in the home service space:

- Monitor business reviews online, such as Google reviews. You can see these reviews when your business is searched on most search engines. You can also see reviews pop up on maps, Facebook, and other online channels.

- Share live videos of your business, your employees, or (when appropriate) your customers. Social media is becoming more and more about video, and adding video to your posts dramatically increases the chances that it will be seen and shared. Unpolished videos are becoming more desirable and trustworthy than those that are too slick or overproduced.

- Provide immediate responses to customer or potential customer comments on your social channels. If you are monitoring your social media effectively, your company's quick and helpful responses show customers how important they are to your business.

- Create interactive posts that encourage participation. For example, posting a question with multiple-choice answers is a good way of getting people to engage with your business. Contests are also a way to encourage people to become active participants on your page, but be careful to follow Facebook rules and guidelines for online contests.

- Upload real-time posts that help customers feel they are there. If you post photos or videos in real time, with content that encourages viewers to be in the moment with you, it can boost your credibility, if done right.

- Take every opportunity to cross-pollinate your social channels with your business news. If you hire a new manager, rewrap trucks, remodel a showroom, or donate money to a worthy charity, not only send out a press release, but post the release on your social pages too, and encourage viewers to share it.

- Speaking of sharing, many people share via instant messaging, text, or email. This can lead to website referrals that are hard to track, creating what is called *dark social*. Although the name sounds somewhat sinister, it is anything but. You want to encourage sharing of your content. It's a fast-growing area of social media, and while it's not trackable, experts agree that it is becoming more popular among social media users, especially those over forty.

- Think about adding a chat service to your website or social media platforms. Chat software is either liked or hated by consumers, but when they make the booking experience better, more convenient, or when the conversation helps the user get the information they need more quickly and easily, it could be a great business builder.

- Paid ads on social media or search engines can expand your business without too much effort. You can boost a Facebook post, buy an ad, purchase AdWords through Google, and much more. Buying ads through these channels has become easier over the years, and by using the tracking tools they provide, you can tailor your ads to a specific target audience, manage the ROI (return on investment) and keep to a budget.

- Use your employees as brand ambassadors to help build your social pages. There has been a lot of back and forth on business social media on whether to ask employees to use their personal social media pages when liking their employer's social media pages. One thing that has been changing is that employers can now see the benefits of having employees share the company's posts with their own social media circles.

USE SOCIAL MEDIA TO VALIDATE YOUR BUSINESS

As mentioned before in this book, news reporters and others in media pay attention to your social media channels, especially if there is a reason for them to check on you or your business. Reporters and media are always looking for an easy story, and if you make it easier for them to get the information or photos they need, the better your chances are to get coverage. And remember, they have deadlines and are working multiple stories at all times, so getting their attention is half the battle.

You may wonder how social media can validate your business. One thing that can be said about social media that can't be said about a business website: if you tell a lie on social media, it's pretty likely you will be called out on it. So those in the media feel a little more secure when checking up on your business news through social media than on a website that is more like a promotional tool than a reality-based platform. A website is not real-time, nor does it have feedback to its pages available for all to see.

So your social media platforms are a way media can investigate your company's credibility without spending a lot of time digging. They can flip through your posts and get a pretty good idea as to whether your product or service is reliable, trustworthy, and responsive. They can also find out if your prices are competitive, if your employees are trained, if your service people are polite and clean, if they clean up after their work is done, if your business stands by its work, and many other factors just by reading your posts and the comments left by your customers on your posts. Facebook also shows customer reviews on your page, so it's easy to see what the comments are, starting with the most recent. Videos that you've posted can reveal whether or not you are comfortable communicating on camera—an important point for a local news outlet that needs experts to interview on TV.

As social media becomes more important to businesses, how your business handles its social platforms will also become more important. Your business might have been around for forty years, but an insensitive or errant social media post can become viral in a very short time, leaving your business in a very vulnerable position. That's a place no business wants to be in, so if social media is an afterthought, it's time to rethink your strategy.

> **As social media becomes more important to businesses, how your business handles its social platforms will also become more important.**

I want to end this chapter with an encouraging message: sometimes the simplest social media messages are the most powerful. One of my clients—a client based in North Carolina—agreed to temporarily use his company's social media page to simply spread a little beauty and joy at the beginning of the COVID-19 pandemic. He directed his service experts to take photos of their trucks in front of anything pretty that they saw. We then posted those photos on social media.

One post featured a photo of the company truck in front of some dogwood trees in bloom—just the truck (with the logo visible) in front of a row of dogwood trees. Another displayed the truck in front of a colorful flower garden. There were photos of the truck with a bright red cardinal sitting above it on a tree branch and in front of a freshly painted mural.

The effects were immediate—and a little surprising. Customers quickly began liking the posts and thanking the business for sharing beauty and joy. But it also made an impact on the technicians. As they looked for new ways to spread this message, they were cheered up and encouraged. The process of engaging them in this way helped reinforce the message that they were all representing the company— that they were all actively working to support the same mission.

This is why social media matters. It's a way to build relationships and to differentiate your business from its competitors.

NEXT
LEVEL
NOW

CHAPTER SIX

Is Your Website Converting Viewers to Customers?

A business owner in the Philadelphia suburbs partnered with Ripley PR to help promote his heating and air conditioning business as the leading home service provider in his market. One of the first steps we take with new clients is to think like their potential customers—or the media—and visit the company's website.

As my team scrolled through the website, they saw information about plumbing services and designed some press release ideas that included promoting the company's plumbing services.

There was only one problem with our calendar of ideas. When we presented it to the client, he interrupted us to say, "We don't offer plumbing yet."

When we explained that it was on his website, he was not pleased with his website company, and we recognized that, before we did any further PR work, we needed to make sure that his website was correct and up-to-date.

Unfortunately, when some digital agencies create a website for a home service business, they use a template. They may switch out the logo and insert your company name and location, but they rely on boilerplate copy for a lot of the site. When your website design was initially approved, you may have focused intently on making sure that the company name, location, and hours are correct, and overlooked the page describing in detail the services you offer.

That's why I want you to think about your answer to this question: When was the last time you had someone you trust read through your website, word for word, checking links and tabs to make sure that all the content is correct? Has it been updated since you expanded your hours, added a new location, or omitted a service that was no longer profitable?

Your website is the world's window into your business. It is often the first impression of you and your business, and it may well determine whether customers call you for that home service they need. Websites of the past were content heavy and almost encyclopedic, causing website visitors to lose interest and leave for less wordy and less boring websites.

Today, your website needs to be fast, easy to read, and include many large visuals. In addition, your call to action needs to be front and center. Your website is your main marketing tool and sales funnel, and if it is difficult to contact your business and the website is cluttered and wordy, potential customers will move on. Keep in mind that your website is likely being viewed on tablets or smartphones, so mobile-friendly websites are a must to capture the client. If your website is not converting website visitors into calls or appointments, it needs work. And if you don't know whether it is or not, you need to find out.

I recommend that every business owner, general manager, marketing manager, or anyone in charge of your company's financial stability and growth have access to your company website's conversion analytics. Simply put, you need to know how many potential customers are visiting your website, which pages they are looking at when they visit, how long they stay on your site, and—the key piece for your sales growth—how many of them actually schedule a service. This will help you understand whether or not the website is doing the job it needs to do.

But first, there needs to be a consensus on what it is you want the website to do. The vast majority of business owners I have worked with want their website to do many things, but at the top of the list is generating leads and calls. Other metrics to track could be how many visitors clicked on a special page for a special offer and filled out a form and submitted it. There are myriad ways to collect these figures and as many ways to present them. Reports, graphs, tables, and spreadsheets are just a few of the ways to track conversions. But you have to decide which numbers you want to collect and what a conversion means to you. Once you have decided what you want to track, then you can use many forms of reporting, and you can choose the kind of report that works best for you.

The best way to start tracking, if you haven't tracked your conversions before, is to look at the history of your website's performance over time. This look back will give you an overview of how the website has performed in the past. This helps to see where you started and gives you a benchmark to use as a point of reference. If you find that there are trends in visitor conversions over the period of a year or two, you can use this information to improve your conversions going forward. In many home service businesses, there are peaks and valleys that correspond to the weather or seasons. Plumbing businesses may see a surge of visitors to their website in the winter, especially if the business is in the northeast. Air conditioning contractors will see a spike in website visitors in the spring and summer. The same seasonal increase in website visitors could be true for businesses specializing in heating and furnace or boiler systems.

The objective of collecting the data from past years is to give insight into when people are most likely to visit your site. But more than that, there are ways to find out what each visitor did once they landed on your website. Many analytic programs exist, but the most used analytical tool, according to Google, is (not surprisingly) Google Analytics (GA). It's a free tool that webmasters can use to track just about every action a visitor takes on the journey through your website.

GA is one of the ways you can find out what your website's conversion rate is. Even better, you control what you want to track, and you can designate how through the dashboard. The basic aspects of GA can be understood by most computer-savvy business people. Meet with your webmaster or digital agency to discuss which metrics you want to track, and they will be able to send you reports regularly (weekly, monthly, or however frequently you need them).

If you have a special offer going on, and there is a link to a specific page on your website from your home page, you can track that. You can see where visitors are from—your city, your county, your state, or even other countries (sometimes through social media links visitors click on your site by accident). You can also follow their path through the website. They may have entered your site from the home page, through a Google search, through a link on another site, or through an online PR promotion like a news article or press release. If you send out eblasts (information or special offers via email) or are active on social media, you can track people who visit your site through those channels as well.

Through GA, you can also find out *how* your visitors are accessing your site. You may be surprised to find out how many people landed on your website via their smartphone or tablet versus a desktop computer. The split is leaning toward smart devices every year, so making sure your website calls to action and lead-generating pages are simple, quick to load, and require minimal typing is essential. Studies show that your website has just seconds to capture a visitor and turn them into a lead or a sale through a well-laid-out funnel that reduces website exits.

Other data to study include what day of the week your site gets the most traffic, what time of day users visit most, how long visitors stay on specific pages, and how many pages a visitor looks at on each visit. Visitor data can be further segmented by age, gender, and—as noted earlier—geographic location and device used to access your website and specific pages.

> **Studies show that your website has just seconds to capture a visitor and turn them into a lead or a sale through a well-laid-out funnel that reduces website exits.**

For instance, do you know how many of your visitors access your website on a hand-held device or a desktop computer? Do you know how many (or what percentage) use iOS or PCs? Of the smartphone users who access your site, are more on Android systems or iPhones? Believe it or not, this data could impact your conversion rates and even how you target those visitors.

If reviewing this data seems complex, it is. But so is getting even one person to go to your website, click on a page, and then buy or select your service or product. You are competing with every other service business in your area if your business services a regional market, or every other similar business nationally or globally if that is your market. Companies like Zappos, Apple, and Amazon are constantly looking at analytics and conversion rates. You need to be doing this too—it's no different than spending time talking with your customers to make sure that you are providing the service they need.

A major reason for collecting or, at the very least, reviewing this data is to find out more about your customers, identifying the patterns that separate visitors from customers, and learning how you can take advantage of those patterns to maximize your conversion rates.

CALCULATE YOUR CONVERSIONS

Let's spend a few minutes doing some basic math. Commonly available conversion rate calculations can help determine how well your website is doing in terms of getting users to take an action after landing on a page on your site.

For instance, if you want to calculate how well your website is collecting leads:

Take the number of leads collected ÷ total traffic on your website × 100 = your conversion rate

Example: 17 leads ÷ 120 traffic × 100 = 14.16%

If you are trying to see if your website is converting visitors into buyers (sales):

Take the number of sales ÷ number of visitors × 100 = your conversion rate

Example: 6 sales ÷ 50 visitors × 100 = 12%

Because conversion rates have become such a hot topic, there are companies that specialize in them. You may see this referred to as conversion rate optimization, or CRO. Much as SEO has become a common term for search engine optimization, CRO is now becoming a term that website developers—and consumers—are using to describe conversion rate optimization. CRO is a highly desired commodity for ecommerce and lead-generation websites.

Companies that offer these services take your website and drill down deep into your lead generation or other specific pages, tapping into the metrics for those pages and investigating the minute details so they can then suggest ways to improve those pages' performance. The end goal is to optimize the correct pages so that the website converts as many visitors into leads or sales as possible.

It's a little easier to collect conversion data for ecommerce sites that sell products, like shoes, clothes, toys, electronics, furnishings, or sports equipment, than to collect data for service business conversions. There are interesting conversion metrics available with a search on Google, and that information is worth reading to help you understand where your business stands in comparison to others globally. However, finding statistics on your competition's website conversion rates is not easy. That's why you may find it helpful to work with a CRO firm that specializes in this area.

The CRO firm Invesp noted in a recent article that conversion rates vary by industry, country, device, platform and more, so finding the average is hard to pin down, even among sellers of the same type of product.[7] But there are statistics that can be found, and according to Invesp internal data gathered from thirty-five lead-generation websites, a conversion rate of about 13 percent for lead-generation websites was the average. Other types of websites convert from 1 percent up to 65 percent and higher.

Most home service businesses would be considered lead-generation websites, so if you do your calculations and find that your lead conversion rate is low, you may want to consider making some tweaks to your website. Other online platforms that link to your website—one example is Google My Business—can also be tweaked to help

---

7   Khalid Saleh, "The Average Website Conversion Rate by Industry," Invesp, accessed November 24, 2020, https://www.invespcro.com/blog/the-average-website-conversion-rate-by-industry/.

improve conversions/lead generation.

Studying and calculating your conversion rate is essential to your public relations and marketing efforts because this data will help you determine if your advertising, media pitching, promotions, social media, or other activities are working. This information is also how you will determine if your calls to action are working.

The good news is that, even if you find that your website visitors are not converting to sales or leads as much or as often as you had hoped, there are many actions you can take to make a big difference in those numbers.

WHAT CAN YOU DO TO INCREASE CONVERSIONS OR LEADS?

I said that it was good news, and I meant it: there are many small things you can do to increase your conversions or leads. The first involves doing a bit of investigation. Enlist the help of a close friend or relative you trust to be a secret shopper on your website before making changes. Have them visit your website and follow a website path you give them, and then ask them if they found it easy, fast, understandable, and efficient to navigate. Next, ask a few other friends to try and schedule a service visit or an estimate and see how those shoppers do on the site. Ask the same questions, but also ask them if they were able to follow a path, if it was obvious, or if they had to spend time figuring things out. Another question to ask the group is if they would write down how much time it took them to get to the desired page, and how many pages they had to visit to get to the destination page. Ask all the secret shoppers what their suggestions are, and remember, it's all in an effort to help find the stumbling blocks to increased leads and increased revenue.

Use the information to really look at your website with a critical eye. Share the results with your team and come up with some suggestions that you think will make your website, the home page, the flow, the call to action, and the end page (like a form for more information, service request, a quote, or a response to a special offer) better and more effective.

Sometimes you can increase your leads with a simple improvement. For instance, what about making the call to action on the home page a different color than the rest of the site? You should always stay with your brand colors, but sometimes a little change on the color of your phone number can make a huge difference in the outcome. The objective is to get people to take action.

If you are nervous about making a permanent change to your website that may actually make matters worse, try a technique many website developers, marketers, and PR agencies use: A/B testing. In the web world, A/B testing is also called split testing or bucket testing. It is basically a way that developers or webmasters test different approaches to a web page, visuals, or content on a specific page.

For example, the existing call to action on your home page may be a box or a starburst shape with a message and a link. If the website has a blue color scheme with an accent color (colors that are in your logo), and your call to action is in a similar blue like everything else, try it in red instead. Your existing page would be the "A" page and the same page using a red call to action would be the "B" page. Just in case you think the color scheme doesn't matter, a study discussed on HubSpot.com noted that a call-to-action button in red beat a green one by 21 percent in conversions.[8] That is incredible, by any standard.

---

8   Joshua Porter, "The Button Color A/B Test: Red Beats Green," HubSpot, accessed November 24, 2020, https://blog.hubspot.com/blog/tabid/6307/bid/20566/the-button-color-a-b-test-red-beats-green.aspx.

I realize that some of these more detailed website practices may be beyond your ability to manage. That's why I recommend using experts to help ensure that your website is providing maximum value. A skilled agency can make a significant difference. During your own A/B tests, the webmaster can direct visitors to either page. Once you have discussed with your webmaster how you want the traffic to the website A/B pages to flow, it will take time to collect statistically viable results. On a high-traffic website, you will need less time, as the pure volume of visitors will allow you to see results pretty quickly. If your website has a small number of visitors, you may want to test for a few weeks, or a few months. Remember to test at a time of year when customers will be most likely to visit your website.

Check the analytics weekly. Examine the differences in traffic flow from one page to the other. If you see that there is a 10 percent increase in clicks on the red call to action, you may want to consider keeping it that way for a while. The great thing about testing your new ideas is that, if they don't work out, you haven't lost much. When you notice that a change hasn't led to the results you want, you can make an almost immediate switch back to what worked.

Let's take a look at some of the easy changes you can test:

- Add or change out the call to action on your home page

- Change the color scheme on a few items

- Add testimonials to your home page

- Add photos of your technicians and team

- Change the position of the call to action (above the fold is best, meaning the content that fills your screen initially when you visit the website)

- Offer a discount, a special code, or a specific percentage or dollar amount off a service

- Test shorter copy versus longer copy (it can make a difference!)

- Make some revisions to your "Contact Us" or "For More Information" lead-generation forms

- Try video on your home page with a link to a special landing page

- Try a different typeface, a bigger size, or different color

These are all examples of simple types of A/B tests you can try. Just reducing the number of fields on your forms could garner amazing results. Some great outcomes have been reported by reducing required fields to three or four rather than the five to ten fields commonly seen.

The bottom line is to test, test, test. Your website is your biggest lead-generation tool, and it should not be treated as a static thing. It should be agile, adjusted and tweaked regularly to generate the traffic and leads your business needs to grow.

NEXT LEVEL

LEVEL

NEXT

CHAPTER SEVEN

Your Reputation Is as Good as Your Last Review

When you operate a home service business, reviews matter. But as far too many of my clients know, customers rarely go online to post a positive review of a successful service visit, a technician who arrived precisely on time, or a bill that was exactly what they expected to pay.

No, customers seldom go online to say something nice; instead, they think about reviewing a business only when they want to post a complaint.

And sometimes it's not just your customers who may post negative reviews. It may be a competitor or even a disgruntled employee.

One of my clients, a home service business based in Indianapolis, encountered this kind of problem when a technician was fired for failing to show up to work on more than one occasion. This young technician created a video in which he complained about his former employer and posted it on Facebook, telling stories about the owners that were completely untrue, and then, at the end, inviting viewers to share the video and to contact him for the same kind of service at a discounted price.

The owners called me after the video had received thousands of likes and been shared dozens of times. They were struggling to understand how one bad employee could cause that much negative attention online. Fortunately, the company had an excellent reputation, and we were able to respond by creating a thoughtful video of the general manager talking about the company in a way that was measured and appropriate.

When people are excited about the service you provide, they may well write a review. Unfortunately, when they're very unhappy, they'll do the same. These reviews show up when potential clients perform a Google search of your business, whether you want them to or not.

You can't control reviews, but it is important to monitor them— and to know when and how to respond. Set up a Google Alert for your brand and for your name as well. Do a Google search of your business regularly to see what new reviews appear. Look at as many review sites as possible, and when you see a new positive review, say thank you. If it's a bad one, answer it honestly and request that they contact you off-line to find a solution.

It's important that customers don't think that their comments or requests for information have fallen into a black hole, so if you can't monitor your social media and reviews daily, you might need to hire an expert who will handle social media and reputation management for your service business. Your reputation could be damaged if customer comments and reviews go unanswered.

Why is that?

Well, when you're going on vacation, you may search for reviews of restaurants and hotels before you make reservations. You probably use the internet to search for reviews more than you realize. Today, you don't even need to search for reviews specifically, because when you do a search online, you will often see reviews and star ratings right under the product or service you've searched.

The numbers prove that reviews matter to potential customers. According to a recent survey by Podium, a whopping 93 percent of people said online reviews have a direct impact on their purchasing decisions. The same survey said that 58 percent of the people surveyed looked at online reviews at least once a week, and

Remember that a key part of PR is building relationships and, as in any relationship, communication matters.

68 percent are willing to pay more for a product or service if they feel confident that they'll have a better experience based on these positive reviews.[9] If your business is not actively seeking loyal customers to write reviews about your service or products, I encourage you to consider that step to take your business to the next level.

There are some rules to follow when it comes to reviews and your business that most professional PR and reputation management firms know about and take very seriously. Remember that a key part of PR is building relationships and, as in any relationship, communication matters. This is not an area to take lightly, and if you are not able to follow through on the suggestions, please make sure you hire an expert to do the legwork on your behalf.

---

9   "The Complete Guide to Online Reviews," Podium, accessed November 24, 2020, https://www.podium.com/resources/podium-state-of-online-reviews/#:~:text=Reviews%20Matter&text=93%25%20of%20consumers%20say%20online,business%20consumers%20would%20engage%20with.

RULE #1: DO NOT BE TEMPTED TO WRITE FALSE REVIEWS OR COMMENTS ABOUT COMPETITORS.

This is a really bad idea, and believe me, it has been tried. It will never turn out well. There is no good reason to do this, not even if your competitors are doing it to you. Ethical businesses do not do this, and starting down this path will lead to nothing but negative results. Take the high road; you will be glad you did.

RULE #2: READ EVERY REVIEW, AND RESPOND PROMPTLY.

There is nothing worse than reading a great review of your business and then responding to it two months after it is posted. First, it's just bad business. If someone takes the time to write a nice review, and your business does not have the time to even read the review or respond, you have just wasted a great opportunity. Second, you have possibly hurt the feelings of someone who is probably a loyal customer. The fact that your business ignored the reviewer for days or weeks creates the impression that you don't care—about the review or the reviewer. Third, by not responding right away, you show everyone reading the reviews that your business is slow to respond.

RULE #3: KEEP IT SIMPLE, SILLY.

There's a reason why you can abbreviate this rule with a KISS. A simple thank-you for a good review is always appreciated. Reviewers like to know the business heard what they said, and a response is validation. As a service business owner, you may be tempted to take reviews of your business personally, especially the ones that are less than favorable. The key to dealing with negative reviews is not to get upset and take a slight as a personal attack. Respond right away, admit fault if that is the case, apologize, and explain that your business is going to address the problem. If necessary, take the conversation off-line by giving the reviewer your email or phone number and asking them to contact you as soon as possible so you can resolve the matter. Don't go into details in the comments area, but always be courteous and businesslike. Never lose your temper. Your goal is to show all customers that you value their business and will respond promptly to concerns.

RULE #4: REMEMBER THAT YOUR RESPONSES WILL BE SEEN BY EVERYONE.

And they could live online for years. Other customers, potential customers, and vendors will have the ability to see your responses, so professionalism is important when crafting your replies, whether the review or comment is good or bad. Never get drawn into a dispute online or a he-said/she-said argument. No one wins when a conversation devolves into a childish fight. Stay professional and never say anything you think you might regret later. A good rule to follow is to never write a response in anger. Cool down first, then let someone else read the response before you post it.

RULE #5: DON'T TRY TO SELL, JUST ANSWER THE QUESTION OR SAY THANK YOU FOR THE COMMENT/REVIEW.

I've seen it too many times: a business responds to an online review with a sales pitch. People are smart, and they can tell when they are being sold to. Don't try that. Pretend you are speaking to a friend, and stick to the subject at hand. If the review or comment is good, say thank you and that you appreciate their business. If the comment or review is bad, apologize for the inconvenience they suffered and let them know you will make it right. That's what people want to hear: that you care and that what they have to say matters.

RULE #6: MAKE YOUR RESPONSE PERSONAL, NOT CANNED.

Do you ever read a series of review responses that all sound the same? It seems clear that the business simply changed a name and copied and pasted their response. That kind of response is possibly worse than no response at all, because no response at least means a customer is not getting a robo-response from a machine. Be careful of trying to automate your responses on social media or online platforms. People are looking for a real person to make a connection with, and your business needs to respect each individual who has reached out. They are important because each potential customer, existing customer, or casual browser can make a difference to your sales through their referrals and through their networks.

These six rules are just the beginning when it comes to maintaining the reputation of your service business. Your company is competing with many others and its reputation matters. Without a good reputation, your business could suffer; a negative impression online could potentially cost you revenue.

HOW DO YOU GET POSITIVE REVIEWS ONLINE?

That is one of the most common questions I am asked by service businesses. It's also one of the most complex questions to answer because there are myriad ways to go about obtaining positive reviews from customers, vendors, and partners.

It all starts with asking.

Many business owners have a hard time with this aspect of marketing their business. Even though your service experts wouldn't have a problem asking a satisfied customer to tell friends and family about their good experience, the mere prospect of asking that same customer to go online and write a review on a website seems more difficult. Most home service business owners realize that word-of-mouth referrals are gold, so make sure your technicians are trained and know how to ask for reviews. You may need to role-play it in your technician training meetings.

Today, it would be hard to imagine making any purchase without seeing a review, either online or on your smart device, when searching for a business or service. So it's an accepted practice to ask customers to write a review if they are happy with your service. It's no longer crossing boundaries to ask for reviews, nor is it being pushy or begging. It might be a little extra work on your part to explain how to write an online review or which platform you recommend to your customers, but it's well worth the effort, as you will see later in this chapter.

Many companies have wholeheartedly adopted reviews as part of doing business; their websites have links to their Google reviews, Yelp reviews, or even Angie's List reviews. If you spend some time searching, you'll see websites with reviews right on the home page, and some with customer video testimonials as well. Some service business websites include photos of satisfied customers with quotes under their photos. Others incorporate entire pages filled with reviews for website browsers to read.

Once you decide to include reviews in your business marketing and PR plan, all it takes is a few to get you started. Ask a friend who has used your service to start the ball rolling. You don't need someone to write a lengthy testimonial or a review that is over the top. Just a sentence saying your business performed well and that the reviewer would hire the business again is sufficient. If none of your friends are customers, think of a customer who told you how happy they were with the work, and give them a call. They will probably be more than happy to help you out by writing a review. But make it easy for them: be sure you have a place where they can go to write the review, along with instructions on how to do it.

Some businesses hand out cards with instructions and steps to follow to write a review, while others have instructions on the business website. You may decide to ask for reviews on every service invoice or have your technicians give out review cards after every call. Other ways to get reviews include Facebook posts encouraging customer reviews, review requests on your business emails or eblasts, and a place where customers can click on your website to leave a written review or testimonial.

THE FLY IN THE OINTMENT

I mentioned how to respond to a bad review earlier in this chapter. While I did explain how to respond to negative feedback, I want to spend just a bit more time candidly talking about how challenging it can be when a customer posts a really bad review. First, to be clear, it's going to happen. However, rather than worry about it, I encourage you to have a plan of action so you are prepared. That way, when it happens (and it will), you will be able to respond in a relaxed, calm manner without taking it personally.

The simple fact about negative reviews is that they will cause damage but not as much as you may think. Reviews mercifully turn over as new ones get posted—that horrible review may not stay at the top of the review results for long. But the best thing your business can do is respond. Respond quickly, professionally, and with only the most genuine concern. As I mentioned earlier, a canned response is not appropriate when you get a really bad review online. Remember, everyone who sees the bad review is also going to see your response. They will see how quickly you responded, how professional your response was, and if you demonstrated care for your customers in the way in which you responded.

The damage from a bad review can be reduced by posting a response that acknowledges what the reviewer said and by assuring the reviewer that your business is committed to making it right. But here's the key point: follow through. So many businesses make an effort in the beginning but fail to follow up on their promises with concrete steps and actions. This can hurt your business if you do not nip it in the bud, so whatever you say your business will do, do it. Ask the reviewer to contact you directly, or connect them with a manager who is responsible for customer satisfaction. Then make sure you find out what the outcome was. If the customer's issue has been resolved, you can ask them to add an update to their review. You could end up with a positive review that started out as a negative.

Bad reviews, while they can often sting, happen all the time. And the public is pretty savvy when it comes to bad reviews. In fact, online users are aware that some negative reviews are fake, and they seem very capable of determining which reviews are real and which are made up. However, when a company takes the time to look into a negative review, it can turn into a positive, according to Vendasta.com. In a recent survey of consumer behaviors, Vendasta.com reported that "if a business resolves its issue quickly and efficiently, 95% of unhappy consumers return to your business."[10]

---

10   Khusbu Shrestha, "50 Stats You Need to Know about Online Reviews," Vendasta, accessed November 24, 2020, https://www.vendasta.com/blog/50-stats-you-need-to-know-about-online-reviews.

Now that's a reason to encourage reviews of your business, watch them closely, and respond right away, no matter whether the review is good or bad.

CHAPTER EIGHT

Make Sure That You Are the Expert

One of my key goals, as a PR professional, is to make sure that your brand is top of mind with TV stations and newspapers. I want to create buzz around your business and ensure that reporters and media will think of you the next time they need an expert source. Good PR helps create Google clout—the more news stories and blogs that position you as an expert, the more influence and status you have on search engines and with media. Being *the* local expert will also lead to invitations to be a guest on television news shows and requests for interviews from newspaper and magazine reporters.

Let me share a recent story to demonstrate how this works. When the EPA announced a phase-out on the production and import of the refrigerant R22 (except for continuing servicing needs of existing equipment) and a ban on the manufacture and installation of new R22 air conditioning or heat pump systems, consumers had questions, and the media needed experts to provide the answers to those questions.

We designed a campaign to position one of my clients as a local authority on the topic, based on a series of what were essentially public service announcements in which my client helped educate the public on older air conditioning systems and what this ban might mean for them during their next service visit. Our goal was to primarily get the attention of local and regional media in Pennsylvania, but soon he was a leading national expert speaking on the R22 phase-out and providing helpful information to a national audience.

Building this kind of expertise is not dependent only on local TV appearances and interviews. National print stories that include your name and quotes in top trade magazines can also increase your credibility on a local level as an established business source—if you leverage the stories locally.

This is the kind of work I do with my clients—finding new ways to help establish them as an authority in their industry. You are an expert in your trade, but if no one knows it, it won't do you much good. That's the goal in this chapter: to coach you about ways to make sure you and your home service business are the experts that the media go to when they are covering a story on your industry or are looking for subject matter experts for a public interest item.

Getting media to come to you for a story doesn't happen easily. It's particularly challenging when there are multiple home service businesses vying for the same coverage in your city or area. Members of the media have many choices for source material and interview subjects when covering stories. My goal is for you to become more attractive to the media than anyone else in your industry in your market. And this is not an overnight process, as you can guess.

So, let's get started. In the next few pages, I'll share my pro tips to help you demonstrate that you are *the* expert—the very best source for information and advice on any topic connected to your business. Even if you have been doing business for thirty years or more, if no one knows your name, you have to start from scratch. There is a strategy to the process of becoming a home service business expert in the eyes of the public, media, vendors, clients, and competitors. As I mentioned, it's not easy, but here are the first steps toward achieving that goal:

PRO TIP: FIX YOUR WEBSITE.

We discussed website strategy earlier in this book, but it's so important that I want to emphasize it again. Your website is often the first thing anyone—media or a potential client—sees after they do a Google search or click on an ad. Would you hire a company to do work in your home these days without looking it up on Google? Spend some time reviewing your website, considering how it might appear to a journalist looking for an expert in your industry. What do they see when they first land on your home page? Is it current? Attractively designed? Is your website easy to navigate? Are there any videos? Testimonials? Calls to action (notice the word *calls* ... not call)? But most importantly, is it professional and do you appear on it? If you want the media and clients to see you as the expert, you need to look like one and project that image at all times.

PRO TIP: START A BLOG.

Your website is your most important PR piece, and it can provide a platform for you to demonstrate your knowledge and expertise. if you do not have a blog on your website, you are missing a huge opportunity to show your expertise and speak directly to homeowners. Your blog does not have to win a Pulitzer, but it must be original content (do not plagiarize), and you need to regularly post informative items that address your customers' needs and concerns. While you can and should mention and educate the reader on your services, the blog is not the place to sell, sell, and sell. When people search for you or your company online, blogs often show up in a Google search, adding to your visibility and credibility. The more authored items that show up in a Google search, the better for you and your company, and the more likely media will see you as a potential expert source.

PRO TIP: GET A FACEBOOK PAGE.

If you are not on social media, you are doing your business a disservice. News reporters and magazine writers all have social media accounts and post often. If they can't find you on social media, you will have a very hard time getting their attention and making sure they know you are relevant and current. If you want to be the expert the media depends on, you must post regularly and often, and offer tips, news, and information about the services you offer. Remember that effective communication depends on engagement and interaction. That means you should follow the news media on their Facebook, Twitter, Instagram, and other social media pages. Think about the reporters you'd like to connect with—the connections you need to build so that they will one day contact you for an appearance or a quote. Make sure you occasionally like their posts or tweets, comment appropriately with compliments on a story, and use hashtags and keywords that will show up in a search. When media want to know what's going on, they will often search hashtags that are relevant to the subjects they write about. And if they see your handle often in their searches, you have already passed the test of relevancy.

PRO TIP: VOLUNTEER OR JOIN GROUPS THAT WILL EXPAND YOUR NETWORK.

Is there a civic group in your town that needs someone with your talents? It may or may not be associated with your industry, but if the group makes decisions or recommendations in your town, it's a good place to start. If you are not the meeting type, think about nonprofits or other organizations in your area where you can meet the people who are influencers in your town. Good bets are Boys and Girls Clubs, YMCAs, Chambers of Commerce, and organizations that help

> The great thing about joining a group or volunteering is that it's a win-win. You increase your visibility in the community, and you are doing good as well.

with food drives or homelessness issues. The great thing about joining a group or volunteering is that it's a win-win. You increase your visibility in the community, and you are doing good as well. Being identified as a helper is a huge benefit when you are trying to become known as a subject matter expert. And the media take notice of your involvement.

PRO TIP: SEND OUT PRESS RELEASES QUOTING YOU AS AN EXPERT.

Media do pay attention to press releases, especially those that are well-written, offer news that has not been shared before, and help them cover a story with the least amount of effort. That doesn't mean they are lazy; it means that all news staff are suffering from the same problem: lack of time and limited staff. If you send a press release that covers a subject that is topical and relevant to the reporter or news staff—especially if it offers a good quote and verifiable facts—the reporter will be more likely to use your press release. Subject matter experts are seen as good sources by both the media and the news-consuming public. According to Nielsen research, perceived expert content has an 88 percent greater impact than branded content.[11] Members of the media know this and will always prefer content that is educational rather than promotional, so when you send your press releases, make sure the content is helpful, or informational in nature rather than self-promoting, to get the earned media coverage you want.

Now that you have started your efforts to become known as a subject matter expert (SME), you want to become more tactical in your approach. It's important to nurture relationships with specific media and publications, particularly those working in your field or industry. One of the ways to get noticed by your peers and solidify your reputation as an SME is to obtain coverage in trade publications for the home services industry in your area of expertise. The more effort you put into this, the better your results will be, so take the time to study the publications relevant to your industry.

A good place to start is to identify the best publications and read them to find out what types of stories get coverage. Study the names of the reporters or journalists who cover stories that are relevant to your business. These are the people you want to follow on social media and via blogs or other news platforms. Many magazines have their own blogs, and print publication writers often contribute content to these online platforms, as well as traditionally through the print magazine or journal. Find out which types of stories they like to cover and create a strategy for each publication.

---

11   "Nielsen: Consumers Crave Real Content When Making Purchasing Decisions," BusinessWire, March 25, 2014, https://www.businesswire.com/news/home/20140325005396/en/Nielsen-Consumers-Crave-Real-Content-When-Making-Purchase-Decisions.

When you're busy, research like this can be daunting. Later in the book, I'll share my recommendations for which parts of your PR campaign can be effectively handled in-house and which you may want to delegate to a PR professional. For now, remember that this is an investment in your business. To be successful, you need to be strategic with your efforts. Follow these steps to plan your tactics for getting your business noticed and quoted in trade and industry publications:

PRO TIP: FIND OUT WHICH PUBLICATIONS ARE THE BEST FOR YOUR BUSINESS AND YOUR GOALS.

If you've been in your industry for years, you no doubt have your favorite trade publications. But I recommend asking some colleagues which ones they read most often. Some have larger circulation than others, so it's good to find out if others are reading the same ones you are.

PRO TIP: READ EACH PUBLICATION FROM COVER TO COVER.

Become very familiar with every publication you wish to appear in. Whether you subscribe to the print edition or read it online, don't just skim the few stories that catch your eye. See what topics are covered often and whom they use currently as subject matter experts, and look for opportunities that may exist for you to be included in future stories.

PRO TIP: KEEP A LIST OF WRITERS YOU LIKE.

If you read a story that appeals to you and it sounds like it could pose an opportunity for your business to be part of a future story, write down the name of the writer, as well as his or her email and social media accounts. Follow them on all their online channels and keep a record of the business experts they currently use. Send them an email with your contact information, a brief description of your background, and your availability as an SME.

PRO TIP: SPEAKING OF PITCHING ...

Usually plan on three months' lead time for any story you want to pitch—that means that you want to pitch an idea for a story at least three months before the deadlines for an issue. Remember, timing your pitches isn't only for story ideas. You could also time your press releases to relate to specific topics on the editorial calendars. Pitching yourself as an SME is much easier when you have published material to use along with your pitch or press release. That's another reason why writing blogs is helpful and a great way to establish your credibility and reliability as an SME.

Think of other ways you can strengthen your credibility and thought leadership. Industry media cover trade shows and conferences, so working with your industry trade group to be included as a speaker at industry events is a great way to boost your visibility. Volunteer to speak, if that is one of your strong suits. Being named on the trade show program as a speaker will ensure that your name appears in print and in the conference's online materials, furthering your authority as an SME. If being a speaker is not possible, see if you can be included on a panel during one of the break-out sessions or workshops. Your name on a program furthers your reputation and clout.

Finally, network with other subject matter experts, even your competition. The saying "Keep your friends close and your enemies closer" has its roots in truth. If you know what your competition is up to, you better your chances of staying ahead of the curve. Not that you want to be buddies and divulge all your business secrets or plans.

But being on good terms with other SMEs in your field can benefit you in many ways. Your trade industry peers and media will see that you are friends with other industry influencers, bolstering your own credibility. If they see that you are willing to trade ideas and business tips with others, you'll be seen as an authority in your industry and someone with connections, rather than someone who is just out for his or her own self-promotion.

Another thing that can help you get coverage in the news is being media trained. This is not to be downplayed, as it is a really important factor when putting yourself out there as an SME. Knowing what to wear, how to sit or stand, and being confident on camera or during an interview off-line can make the difference between getting called by the media and being passed over for someone who is easy to work with. In fact, media training is so vital that I want to spend the next chapter coaching you on this critical skill.

As I mentioned earlier in the chapter, media have a tough job, and most newsrooms are stretched. You always want to take steps to make their job easier—that's the key to being an SME that gets called on for an interview or to give quotes or sound bites for news stories. The better you are at working with the media, the more likely they will be to want to work with you.

NEXT LEVEL
NOW

CHAPTER NINE

Media Training Matters

Every media interview is an opportunity to tell a story.

That story should always be the one *you* want to tell. You can use that opportunity to introduce new customers to your company, present yourself as an expert, and describe the things your business does well. It's an opportunity to sell your on-time and friendly service and your highly trained and knowledgeable service experts.

That's why I say that media training matters. You don't want to waste those opportunities. You want to be prepared with strong answers, you need to practice to get comfortable with the format, and you should always plan a strategy to leverage media appearances into a larger campaign to support your goals.

The majority of the stories about companies that you see in the news were pitched to journalists by a PR agency like mine. We create those opportunities by reaching out to journalists and pitching ideas for stories. PR pros outnumber journalists six to one.[12] That means they're inundated. You have to really be savvy to get a story published—and to craft a pitch that stands out.

These opportunities may be planned well in advance, or they may result from an unexpected event or weather shift. You want to be prepared, because it can and does happen: a deep freeze is forecast in the area, and none of the local plumbers have a PR agency working to position them as experts with the media. In those cases, a journalist may Google local plumbing businesses and start calling businesses just like yours, asking, "Hey, can we go with you on a service call to repair a homeowner's frozen pipes?"

Sometimes, companies are approached by the media because of a problem or crisis. In the next chapter, we'll talk in more detail about how to respond to a business crisis, but for now, my goal is to share the techniques I use with my clients to help them successfully navigate interviews and appearances designed to create positive press for their company.

I want all my clients to be proactive. I have the same goal for you. That's why I'm sharing my tips now, before you need them, and encouraging you to practice and prepare so that you're ready. It's not something you should put off until you have the opportunity; you need to always be prepared.

I recommend media training to my clients as a key step at the very beginning of our working relationship. When a client comes on board with us on a retainer, meaning that we're their public relations agency of record and we're going to be acting on their behalf, one of the first things we do is offer media training to the owner and

---

12   Mike Schneider, "Report: PR Pros Outnumber Journalists by a 6-to-1 Ratio," PR Daily, September 19, 2018, https://www.prdaily.com/report-pr-pros-outnumber-journalists-by-a-6-to-1-ratio/.

anyone who may be asked to speak on behalf of the company. It happens before they have a story—before we know precisely how and when we want to pitch opportunities to journalists. Our goal is that, after the high-level media training we do with clients, they feel good about their expertise and how to demonstrate it. We want them to be prepared, to feel ready to talk about their business confidently.

A few of my clients have been transformed into—well, I hate to call them "media stars," but they are on TV constantly, whether they're part of a discussion on preparing your home for a specific season, or a story about water heater safety, or some other newsworthy topic connected to residential service. No matter how often they've done this, we like to make sure that their preparation includes tips on what to discuss. When you have an opportunity to speak to the media, your goal should always be to communicate a few key facts about your company, the facts that distinguish you from your competitors and emphasize that you are experts in your industry. Three is a good number—three points you want to make, three tips you'd like to share, or three things you'd like to highlight about your business.

You don't want to write out a script. It's not interesting to hear someone just recite some memorized lines. It should be conversational, as if you were talking with a real person, a real customer, and sharing your knowledge with them. Your three tips should really be bullet points, reminders of the key information you'd like to share.

I say that it's like talking to a customer because, in my experience, if you are a good salesperson for your business, you have a talent for making other people feel comfortable. And those are the same skills you can use for a successful media appearance. When you work in the home service business, you are spending time in people's homes. You're asking questions about them, about their family, things like "Does your child have asthma?" "Does anyone in your family have indoor allergies?" and "What will make your home more comfortable?" That kind of warm and friendly approach is exactly what's needed here and will provide a strong foundation for the high-level tips I'll share in this chapter. If you service a home in any capacity, these skills will help you.

LIGHTS, CAMERA, ACTION

It may seem obvious, but there's only one way to get comfortable speaking on camera, and that's by using a video camera to record yourself speaking and then watch the recording.

Most of our agency clients are not based near our office, so we don't always get to do media training in person. But if we can, we like to bring in a video camera and conduct a mock interview. We ask questions, they respond. Then, we look at the recording, and ask the client, "What do you think you could have done better?"

Our clients are usually surprised, often unpleasantly, at what they see. They say things like: "I talked too long." "I kept shifting in my seat." "I touched my face a lot." "I kept saying 'um.'"

We are all accustomed to seeing interviews with performers, sports figures, politicians—people who spend a lot of time in the public eye. They generally make these interviews seem effortless, but what seems effortless is most likely the result of many hours of training to appear at ease and comfortable.

I encourage you to try it now for yourself. If possible, ask a friend or family member to be your interviewer, and prepare your list of three points you'd like to communicate. Give them a few questions to ask based on these points, and then sit down in front of the camera and record this practice interview.

Now, take a careful look at your performance. Is your posture good? Do you seem relaxed? Are you speaking clearly and confidently? Did you communicate the points you wanted to make?

One client I've worked with for years is a wonderful guy who operates a very successful plumbing business in the Nashville area. He originally came to me after he had just done a media appearance; he brought a copy of the video with him to our first meeting and played it for me.

The first thing I noticed was that, throughout the entire interview, he stood with his hands in his pockets and he kept rocking back and forth. It's a posture that's completely natural—except when you're on camera. I was cringing as I watched this very skilled professional become less authoritative on camera with every passing second. Oh, and, even though he wasn't chewing it, it was obvious he had gum in his mouth throughout the interview.

When the video ended, this client turned to me with a big smile and asked, "How did I do? Be honest!"

I always try to give feedback to clients in the most positive, tactful way, so we spent some time talking specifics about body language and posture. Then, we practiced with a mock interview, and then another, and another after that. It took some time and effort—at first, he overcorrected, and stood very stiffly to avoid the temptation to sway—but that practice paid off, and he's now on TV all the time. The media love him, in part because he's perfected the ability to be natural and relaxed on camera.

Since I'm talking about the importance of avoiding unnecessary movement, let me add a warning here about studio chairs. TV studios often have tall swivel chairs on set for interviews. I'm not sure why they are so common, but we spend a lot of time working with clients to avoid the temptation to swivel back and forth. There's something instinctive about it—if a chair moves, you want to move it. But it's incredibly distracting on camera.

As you practice and review your performances, pay attention to your posture. Try crossing and uncrossing your legs or ankles, and then note the difference in how each appears on camera. When you cross your legs, be sure to cross them toward the interviewer. Practice sitting on a chair and then a couch, and do the same assessment. Next, practice standing. Record yourself outdoors and indoors and note these differences. And never cross your arms—you want to appear open in conversation, not closed off. Ask a trusted friend or family member to watch the recordings with you and share their honest feedback.

> Surface impressions matter, but your media appearance is an opportunity to tell your story, so you want to pay as much attention to *what* you say as to how you say it.

Of course, this is only the beginning. Surface impressions matter, but your media appearance is an opportunity to tell your story, so you want to pay as much attention to *what* you say as to how you say it.

TAKE A BREATH

When you're being interviewed, when you're asked a challenging question or thinking about the points you want to make, it can be tempting to respond quickly.

I remind my clients to first take a breath.

Whether the interview is live or prerecorded, whether you're being interviewed via Zoom, by phone, or in person, it's always good to pause before you respond.

Watch an interview with someone who spends a lot of time on camera, and you'll see the value in this pause. It suggests that the person being interviewed is thoughtful, is considering the question, and is thinking before responding.

It's okay to wait before answering, to really think about your response. That pause gives you an opportunity to gather your thoughts, to prepare to speak clearly and communicate whatever it is you want to say.

It's also okay to request that the interviewer repeat a question or rephrase it if you don't understand what they are asking.

It's also absolutely okay to admit that you don't know the answer. If you're not sure, don't pretend, and never make up an answer. Simply say that you don't have that information now but will do your best to find out. And then follow up when you have the information they've requested.

TELL YOUR STORY

In an interview, the words you use matter. A journalist may spend an hour talking to you, and the end result may be only a few seconds on air or a short quote in an article. Every second that you're speaking is important. For that reason, you should always focus on who you are and what your business does—not what it doesn't do.

Compare these two quotes:

"We don't offer plumbing; we only offer heating and air conditioning."

"Our business offers 24-7 emergency heating and air conditioning service and will refund 100 percent of your service if you aren't satisfied."

Do you see the difference? In the second quote, the message is positive, and conveys facts that differentiate the business from its competitors. This should be your goal. Always say what you do, not what you don't do. You also never want to mention your competition, either positively or negatively. Your goal is to tell *your* story, not someone else's.

While you want to be friendly and approachable, it's important to keep in mind that this is not a conversation with a friend. We encourage our clients to think of a media appearance as a sales call. It's not a conversation; it's a transaction. This interaction has a purpose, and you'll want to keep that purpose in mind as you prepare. What do you want people to know about you and your business? What are your goals—how will you know that this appearance was successful?

Think about what makes your story interesting and unique. Let's say that your grandfather started your home service business in 1930, and you are now the third generation operating a business that has become a real fixture in your community. You want to tell that story in your interview. Don't say, "We've been around for ninety years." Instead, start with a little bit about that history: "My grandfather started Downey Plumbing in 1930 with a borrowed Ford Model A pickup truck; today, we have a team of seventy-five skilled technicians."

Carefully consider the key points you want to make and practice a few bridging words or phrases to lead the interview toward the message you want to deliver. If you're wondering what bridging words are or how to use them, spend a few minutes watching a skilled politician being interviewed on the news or participating in a political debate, and you can see this in action. No matter the question, a gifted politician is always able to lead the conversation back to his or her key message using a few bridging words—words that preserve the flow by forming a connection between two separate ideas.

This definitely requires practice, because it needs to sound natural, not forced. Remember that your goal is to communicate a few key points within the context of any interview.

BRIDGING WORDS YOU CAN USE

Practice these bridging words to lead a question or interview in the direction of the points you want to communicate:

"That's a great question! I've also found that my customers are especially interested to know ... "

"We haven't seen that in our business. In fact, when I talk to our customers ... "

"That is certainly a problem, but what we see even more often is ... "

"I haven't experienced that, but what I have encountered is ... "

"We expect that to be an issue in another year or two, but right now, what we are focused on is ... "

Communication also depends on clarity, so try to avoid industry jargon, or abbreviations that are commonly used in your business but may not be known to customers. If you're discussing "bleeding a pipe" or referring to "air changes per hour," briefly explain what this means.

DRESS LIKE A PRO

When you're representing your business in a media interview—especially if you're going to be on camera—it's critical to dress professionally. If you usually wear a uniform, wear it. If you have a nice polo or button-up shirt with your logo on it, wear that.

Don't put on a suit if you don't normally wear a suit to work. But if you normally wear a T-shirt and jeans, you may want to put on a button-down shirt instead.

Your clothing can communicate in a way that either confirms or distracts from your message. If your goal is to demonstrate professionalism and competence, the clothes you wear should support that message.

We recently had the wonderful experience of highlighting a client's support of her community's homeless shelter. It was a charity that she had donated generously to for several years; we wanted to make sure that her community knew about this support. We pitched an interview to the local news station and invited them to talk to her about her donation of $25,000. My client is very smart, but still this was an opportunity to remind her to be thoughtful about what she wore to the interview so as not to distract from her message. That means no expensive designer handbags and no flashy jewelry.

Sunglasses are another no-no. People want to see your eyes; it's a way to communicate trustworthiness. If you're being interviewed outside on a sunny day, simply walk over to a shady area for the interview and remove those sunglasses.

IT'S NOT ALL BAD

Some of the business owners I have spoken with have the perception that the media is out to get them—that if they agree to an interview or an appearance, they'll be the victim of "gotcha journalism" or be tripped up by a trick question. I remind them that the kind of preparation we are doing is designed to equip them to be a valuable expert source. When we pitch a story and line up an interview, the journalist doesn't have an agenda. Their goal is not to ask tough questions; their goal is to provide their readers or viewers with helpful information.

Keep in mind that the focus of this chapter is on positive PR and how to work with the media to tell your story. Crisis management—how to respond to the media when your business encounters a problem—is a very different process and one which I'll discuss in more detail in the next chapter.

We spend a lot of time working with clients to develop tips and techniques to use to anticipate the questions they'll be asked—even tough questions. I encourage you to try some of these on your own. It can be challenging to anticipate tough questions, so do some research. Look at interviews of other home service pros and study the questions they're asked. Think about how you might respond if the same question were asked of you.

Reflect on any problem areas, and consider how to respond to a question connected to them in a positive way. For example, maybe you've lost several of your best technicians to a competitor this year. Instead of saying, "That company poached my best workers," you might want to say, "We've been streamlining all aspects of our business this year to deliver the best value for money to our customers."

A media appearance is an opportunity to demonstrate your expertise, to talk about your business to potential clients, to highlight what's unique and important about the work you do.

As I mentioned earlier, if you don't know the answer, be honest. Admit that you don't have a response in that moment but will give them one as soon as you can.

MAKE EVERY OPPORTUNITY COUNT

A media appearance is an opportunity to demonstrate your expertise, to talk about your business to potential clients, to highlight what's unique and important about the work you do. I encourage you to practice the skills I've discussed in this chapter—you can use them not only for interviews and appearances, but in any situation in which you are representing your business and selling the services you offer.

I want to close this chapter with a few final quick tips that you can practice today to equip yourself for that next opportunity:

- *Say no to "yes/no"*: Nothing is duller than an interview in which the only responses are "yes" and "no." You're not on trial; you're telling a story. Use full sentences to do it.

- *Speak in sound bites*: Speaking in full sentences is good because the media are looking for a good quote or two to round out the story. Make sure to say your business name two or three times in the course of your interview. Instead of always saying "I" or "we," try something like "At Marco Plumbing, our focus is ... "

- *Pay attention to the interruption*: If the reporter seems to be interrupting you, it may mean that your answers are too long or you're talking too much. Try shortening your answers a bit and make sure that you're directly answering the question that's been asked.

- *Remember that you're the expert*: It's normal to be nervous, but you know your business better than the journalist or reporter. Practice and prepare, and then be confident!

CHAPTER TEN

Are You Prepared for a Business Crisis?

You get a call on the weekend informing you that one of your technicians has been arrested for driving under the influence while operating a company truck.

A customer files a police report claiming that jewelry has been stolen from her home, and she accuses the employee who made a service call to her home earlier that day.

Your company was featured in an undercover sting story by a local investigative reporter.

You discover that your best technician is starting a competing business, and has been contacting your customers, offering the same services for less.

No matter who you are or how successful your business is, at some point you will face a crisis. It doesn't mean that you did something wrong. It may not be your fault at all. It may be that a process broke down, an employee became disgruntled, or simply that someone made a mistake.

One of the most important assignments I have as a PR professional is to help my clients navigate crises, and after years in the business, I've learned that crises always happen. The secret is to prepare in advance so that, when a problem arises, you are ready. When your business or your reputation are threatened, especially by circumstances beyond your control, it's natural to feel emotional, even angry. But if you're prepared for the crisis in advance, you won't simply *react*—you can *respond* thoughtfully and responsibly.

I talk to my clients about having a crisis plan early in our relationship because I want them to have the tools and strategies in place ahead of time—and I want the same for you. That's why I'll share here some of the advice we give to our clients, the heart of the crisis plan we develop long before there's a crisis to which they need to respond.

BE CRISIS CONSCIOUS

A goal for your crisis plan should be to prepare in advance for potential crises that could occur. I call that being *crisis conscious*. This means identifying any potential vulnerabilities in your operations and being thoughtful about how you might respond. You can get started by paying attention to any crises that arise in your business community and considering how you might respond to similar challenges. Here are a few sample questions you'll want to be prepared to answer:

- What will you do if your customer database is hacked and sensitive billing information is no longer secure?
- How will you respond if equipment is installed improperly and the home catches on fire?

- What actions will you take if a dissatisfied customer posts negative comments on social media?
- Which steps will you take if a terminated employee files a lawsuit?

GET READY

A crisis plan helps you to prepare for most possibilities. The goal is to put in place steps to take if an unexpected setback or disaster occurs.

Your company's future and survivability depend on swift and effective communication through as many channels as possible to avoid the whiplash that many companies and individuals suffer in a crisis. If you don't have a plan in place, sit down and hash it out, or hire experts in crisis planning. You don't want to be surprised by a crisis and then have to decide how best to respond.

You can read it in the headlines almost every day: businesses and brands are suffering. You don't want this to be you or your business. Protecting your reputation, your revenue, and your employees and customers are all key elements of an effective crisis plan. And that requires preparation, and thinking ahead, before a crisis exists.

Protecting your reputation, your revenue, and your employees and customers are all key elements of an effective crisis plan. And that requires preparation, and thinking ahead, before a crisis exists.

If you neglect to prepare and then don't respond appropriately, it may not cause the complete failure of your business, but it can create a lot of unnecessary headaches and embarrassment. I've learned many lessons from years of helping clients through various crisis situations. Here is a list of the top things not to do when faced with any kind of crisis:

1. Do not assume it will just go away. Immediate action is the key to helping a crisis fade away quickly.

2. Do not try to shift responsibility to someone or something else; if you are the one in charge, it is your problem, and you need to fix it.

3. Do not point fingers or claim someone else made you do it; the best way to repair a tarnished reputation is to demonstrate competence and professionalism.

4. Do not downplay the severity of the situation; even if it's not the end of the world, your clients or customers often feel that it is. Apologize sincerely.

5. Do not feign concern or alarm; you must show authentic feelings and deep caring for the blunder that you or your business created. People can sniff out a lame response, and you and your business will be called out for it.

6. Do not bury your *mea culpa* in a flurry of other online or media responses; get the apology out on every platform available, and repeat it multiple times. Put it on Facebook, Twitter, your website, blogs, and in your responses to media. (A note here to make sure that your attorney reviews any public apology before it is posted—crisis statements should always be reviewed by your legal advisor for your protection. There are times when an apology may not be appropriate.)

7. Do not respond with a knee-jerk reaction; if you do, you will regret it. While you do need to respond immediately, remember to do it calmly and professionally. Your responses

could live online forever, and being on the list of top year-end business flops is not where you want to be.

If your service business has never been in a crisis situation or has never experienced a disaster (no matter how big or small), consider yourself lucky. But just because you have avoided a crisis thus far, it does not mean you can rest on your laurels.

A crisis can happen in a split second and without warning. And no business is immune. You may have already experienced a business crisis without even knowing it. I want to equip you to deflect or correct an issue before it becomes a true crisis.

WHAT MAKES A CRISIS A CRISIS?

Think back and examine past situations that could have escalated into a crisis. How did you fix them? Was your response immediate, or did it take a while to decide what to do?

Here are just a few of the problems your business may experience that can quickly escalate into a major crisis situation:

- A customer feels your business took advantage of them, and they complain online or directly to the media

- An employee feels they were treated poorly and posts about it on social media

- An employee is badly injured on a job site

- An ex-employee targets the business in a violent rampage

- An employee is accused of stealing (from the business or a client)

- An employee is caught doing something wrong on video

- The business makes a false statement or makes a flub on social media (this happens more often than you think)

It's important to acknowledge that businesses are more visible than ever before, especially if you are operating in someone's home. Increasingly, homes are equipped with video and security cameras and audio monitoring devices. Your technicians are likely being watched remotely on service calls. Social media (even your business platforms) adds to this visibility, because what you say on social media could follow you for years. Any of the above could happen without warning. And given the nature of online platforms and social media, it takes seconds for a complaint or bad behavior to become the next viral video circulating in your town, or worse, around the nation or world.

Good things happen that can be shared all the time, of course, but it is the bad stuff that gets the attention. If your company helps an animal shelter find homes for dogs, that's a good thing, and maybe it could become a human-interest story with the right PR, but if a technician is videotaped mistreating a client's pet while on a call, that is a disaster.

How do you know when a situation is about to become a crisis? Savvy business owners have a good instinct for this, I've found. When you get that feeling in your gut, when you see the video or social media post, or when someone comes to you and says, "Hey, did you know … " you'll likely sense that a small problem is about to balloon into a crisis. Another tip-off is when the news crew shows up at your business address asking questions.

Nothing is worse than being taken by surprise or being unprepared. That is why having a PR crisis plan is not a *should-have*, it's a *must-have*. Today's world moves so fast that, without a plan, your business is at risk in many more ways than it has ever been. We all know that being transparent is the buzz word for businesses, but with transparency comes a little bit of fear, right? Most service businesses are in a highly competitive market, and while you want to have a transparent business, you also don't want to give away the baby with the bathwater. It's a challenging conundrum and requires finesse to strike just the right balance.

A reputable PR agency that specializes in home service businesses knows where to draw the line and can develop a master plan for your brand and what to do when a crisis occurs (or is about to occur). Obviously, avoiding a crisis in the first place is the preferred plan, but disasters or fiascoes generally happen out of the blue or in an instant, and with very little warning.

WHAT DOES A PR CRISIS PLAN DO?

First and foremost, a PR crisis plan will save you and your business precious time and effort. That can be a significant advantage if and when a crisis occurs. The main objective of a crisis plan is to help you and your business remain calm in the face of a potentially damaging event or situation.

The main objective of a crisis plan is to help you and your business remain calm in the face of a potentially damaging event or situation.

While you cannot address each and every potential crisis in one plan, it is possible to create an overarching plan to manage most issues your business could encounter. The basics of a crisis plan are the following:

- *Create an employee crisis tree.*

  Decide in advance who will be responsible. That means identifying the answers to these questions: Who talks to media? Who messages on social media? Who liaises with your team? Who manages website updates and content throughout the crisis?

- *Have press statements created and approved.*

  If your business finds itself in a crisis, an immediate press statement is always a good idea, and while social media is the first line of defense today, a well-thought-out press statement with critical information can always help. Have the crisis contact names and phone numbers on the press release, as well as the location where updates and media information will be available. Facebook and Twitter are typical platforms where immediate information can be disseminated. Just be sure that the person responsible for posting is trained in social media communication and crisis.

- *Have a social media rollout plan.*

  Timing is everything, so having a plan set up for how often and where news updates will be offered to the public is necessary. Every thirty minutes? Every hour? As needed? It will help media to know who to reach out to and what numbers to call for more in-depth information. Social media is a good way to connect and stay linked to media.

- *Designate a staffer who is media trained to speak on camera.*

  Media training is no luxury these days; I discussed some of the key skills necessary for media appearances in the previous chapter. I recommend that every business owner be media trained for an emergency or crisis. Media will want to interview someone who is calm, stable, knowledgeable, and helpful for on-camera appearances. Beauty or attractiveness are not necessary attributes for on-camera effectiveness. Instead, training and genuine sincerity will matter more on camera.

- *Produce a coordinated communication map.*

  The balancing act between complete truth and being forth-coming can be tough in a crisis situation. Sometimes a business can't be 100 percent transparent when there are delicate or legal issues at stake. But your crisis plan should articulate how transparent your spokespersons and social media accounts can be. And there must be coordination so that each communi-cator (the media spokesperson, the owner, the management team, the PR person, the social media person, and so on) is on the same exact page.

- *Experiment with and test your plan.*

  Practice always matters, and in a crisis, it's absolutely vital. Unless you are a professional PR crisis management firm, or have hired one, you'll need to find out if your plan is going to work as expected. Are the media representatives you have on your list the ones that are the best fit to get the word out? Are the employees you have designated for crisis plan positions ready to perform their duties? Is your social media plan up-to-date and current? Have you identified the right industry influencers who will be conduits for getting your messaging out into the public? Does everyone know their place in the crisis plan and are they comfortable performing their tasks?

MAKE YOUR RESPONSE COUNT

When a crisis happens, when your business is threatened, it's natural to feel emotional. There's a lot of anxiety and stress. It can be difficult to think on your feet.

I discussed media appearances in the last chapter; there, the focus was on creating opportunities for positive PR. But when your business faces a crisis, when the media contacts you for a response or to answer questions, it's especially important to tell your side of the story in a way that is respectful, firm, and thoughtful.

We work with clients to help them prepare, to understand that an investigative journalist may ask challenging questions designed to prompt a quick and heated response. A key part of the preparation is to create a written statement in advance. This statement should be reviewed carefully, possibly by an attorney, to ensure that it accurately communicates your message.

This statement can then be shared with all appropriate media outlets. It can be posted on your social media. It can be referred to or offered whenever your business is contacted for a response. It ensures that your message is consistent, correct, and accurate.

Nothing is ever off the record. If you say it in front of a journalist, you should prepare for it to be in the story. Saying "No comment" can give the appearance of guilt. We usually recommend that our clients always have a response prepared.

Finally, you will need to have a team member monitor the overall crisis coverage and company messaging for correctness and effectiveness throughout. This person (or persons) will not only watch the overall effectiveness of the plan but will also be responsible for managing the comments and questions being posted online. This person will measure the climate of the online community to the crisis and how the business is handling it in the eyes of all interested parties, whether customers, vendors, stakeholders, or the public. This is actually one of the most important aspects of a crisis plan and is all too often overlooked.

The person or persons measuring the effectiveness of the messaging and measuring the online climate through the comments, responses, likes, and shares will need to have a direct line of communication with the top executives and CEO, to make sure they know what the public is saying and feeling about the crisis and the business's response to it. Without monitoring the community's response (including all members of the community: media, vendors, clients, public, competitors, etc.), a crisis plan can't be deemed effective. And if tweaking needs to happen, you'll want a person who is on top of it on all channels.

If this seems like a lot of work, it is. It's also essential that whatever you decide to do—whether creating your own response or hiring a PR crisis management agency—you need a plan before a crisis happens. If you don't have one, you could be risking your company's very survival when a crisis or tragedy occurs.

NEXT LEVEL

CHAPTER ELEVEN

Can You Do It In-House?

Home service companies are good businesses. Many owners I know run successful operations with revenue in the millions of dollars.

You don't reach that level of success without understanding how to market your business and how to sell your services to customers.

Businesses like these—and like yours—are equipped to promote the work they do. You may have a dedicated marketing person responsible for promotion and communication. You may have an events coordinator to manage home shows or arrange appearances in local parades.

But as we discussed at the beginning, successful PR is different from advertising. It's not the same as promotion. It's understanding how to tell your story in a way that is engaging.

Many service business owners think PR is all about touting how much you've given to charities, announcing your new general manager, or introducing a new service line. Easy enough, right? But it's a lot more than that. Good PR can mean the difference between struggling to increase your revenue and attract the best technicians in your market on the one hand and being able to take your hands off the steering wheel and concentrate on managing all these areas of your business on the other.

There is a reason why there is an entire industry dedicated to public relations. It's definitely not a do-it-yourself project to try out when your livelihood (not to mention your employees' livelihoods) depends on it. In the past, service businesses were able to squeak out the basics by sending traditional press releases about a new office location or service offering or using paid advertising to get the word out about their business. This approach will not work today.

I've shared tips and techniques in the past few chapters to encourage you to be thoughtful about how to present your business effectively. These are basic steps you can take in-house, and I share them freely.

But ultimately, if you truly want to grow your business to the next level, hiring a PR professional is the best investment you can make. Spend a few minutes considering these eight points, and decide how they may apply to your business:

1. *Your time is valuable.*

   It's true that, as a business owner, your time is critical to your company's success. You need to focus on making your business grow, obtaining more leads, following up with potential new revenue opportunities, and managing your company's financial health. PR professionals with experience and knowledge of the service industry already know how to make connections with the most important influencers. We know what types of stories will get their attention. When you think about what your time is actually worth, you'll see that it's much more cost-effective to let experienced professionals do the leg work for you.

2. *Your employees aren't trained to manage your brand.*

Brand awareness is a big part of any PR plan. How many members on your team are experienced in branding and PR? If your service business is like most, you do not have a dedicated reputation expert on staff. You may have a marketing specialist, but this does not mean they truly understand public relations. PR is very specialized; the best PR agencies have employees who have many years of experience promoting and leveraging brands. You want the best and most experienced technicians on your team; shouldn't the same be true for the PR professionals who manage your brand?

3. *How will you handle a PR crisis?*

Crisis management is undoubtedly one of the most critical parts of your PR planning. I've talked about it a lot in this book for that very reason. Hopefully, you won't ever have to deal with a public relations crisis involving your service business. But when you manage a business, you don't have the luxury of wishful thinking or lack of adequate preparation. It's a lot like not getting car insurance and hoping you won't get into an accident. You may avoid a crash for many years. On the other hand, your son could back your truck into the garage door tomorrow. That's the risk people take when driving without insurance. It's the same when you postpone thinking about—or preparing for—a PR crisis. Consider having a PR professional review your business and develop a crisis plan in the event of an unforeseen event. Your goal should be not simply to be proactive in the event of a crisis but to prevent an incident or problem from ballooning into a crisis. A crisis can hurt your reputation for a very long time.

Having a professional plan can help you avoid much of the aftermath that follows.

4. *Getting earned media attention takes effort.*

I have discussed the importance of earned media coverage in previous chapters, but it bears repeating. Earned media is a far better way to achieve attention than through traditional advertising channels. True, a nice TV commercial, radio spot, or flashy print ad might generate interest and funnel calls to your business. But what medium do consumers trust the most when they want to find out about a company or business? News stories and online reviews beat out ads in survey after survey. Earned media attention doesn't just happen. It takes dedicated effort and a lot of time. Public relations firms with experience in gaining earned media attention for service businesses know the best ways to court the media, can identify who the best contacts are, and are familiar with which publications need a story, what subjects they cover, and the kinds of stories that capture their attention. It takes time to develop these contacts, and a professional PR agency with experience and a solid reputation in your industry could be well worth considering and may offer the best return on your investment.

5. *Social media presence is a necessity.*

If you think social media just means posting sales pitches on Facebook every day, you are missing an opportunity to build and strengthen relationships with customers and potential customers. Too many businesses don't make social media management a priority within their company. Social media should be a key piece in your business strategy; it's not a job for amateurs. But who on your staff is qualified to supervise, or actually manage, social media for business? Having a personal social media account does not mean someone is an expert in social media. The posts that ensure that your social media pages support your business goals have virtually nothing to do with the pictures or messages that garner likes on someone's personal pages. Social media is a term that is misunderstood by many businesses, because it is a very broad term that covers so many media channels. But the takeaway here is this: your business social media accounts need to be managed and monitored by an expert. Not once a month, when a busy employee has a few minutes, but every day, sometimes even every hour. Why? Because anything can happen in an hour. What if a client posts on your Facebook page that the technician left large muddy shoe prints all over their new carpet? What if no one gets back to them? What if someone answers them, telling them that someone will call, and no one ever does? Every other person who follows your page could potentially see this interaction, and the reaction may not be good. Calm, professional interactions are needed, along with solid follow-up. Professional PR agencies know exactly how to handle your social media.

6. *Your word is not your bond—not anymore.*

Remember when a handshake was all that was needed to seal a deal? Businesses operate very differently today. When was the last time you trusted the word of a hotel website when it came time to make a reservation? You didn't believe the hype you read on the hotel website, did you? You know why? Because you are like everyone else. You want to know what people who have actually been there have to say about it—you read the reviews and comments and then decide whether or not to book a room. It's okay. I do it too. I check TripAdvisor reviews, Google reviews, hotel reservation site reviews, and anything I see on a Google search before I commit. It's the same for your business. Your website might have great testimonials on it, but potential customers want more. They want to see real-time reviews from third-party sites. They will Google your business name and check for comments and feedback from customers, and inevitably, negative reviews will be the ones they check the most carefully. What that means for your business is this: you need to monitor and manage your online reputation. This is not simply a matter of monitoring your social media posts and the comments posted on your Facebook page. This requires a dedicated person who pays attention to all the mentions they see about your business online. How many stars are attached to your business on a variety of review sites? What appears first when a customer types your business name into a search engine? How can you get satisfied customers to write complimentary reviews on review sites? Who will keep track of all this and create and manage reports so you can have a way to get an overview of your company's reputation? You cannot leave this to chance anymore, so hiring a professional who knows the best way to manage your reputation is key.

7. *You can't promote your business alone.*

And maybe it's best not to. Let me take a moment and speak to you frankly. You might think you are the best person to promote your brand or your service business to the world. You may be wrong. You may not be the best person to deal with media. You may not be your own best representative when it comes to telling your story. It's hard to hear, but I've seen it happen far too often. A service business owner gets a reporter to finally come and do a story on the business, and the interview goes south, or the story never sees airtime, or the business comes across in an unfavorable light. It's a gamble if you are not media trained. It really is an art when working with reporters. The smallest things can undercut your message, especially if you are nervous, distracted, or unprepared. You need a partner who can teach you the intricacies of working with the media. A professional PR agency in the home service industry already knows which types of stories interest the local media, which are of national interest, and what reporters want to know. Being prepared is a huge part of the interview process, and a professional PR agency can guide you in every aspect of TV appearances, whether for a breaking news story, special interest coverage, or a guest spot on a TV special or news show.

8. *You need a leg up on your competition.*

Do you have an employee who evaluates your competition? In a perfect world, your business should be watching their activities, monitoring their social media periodically, reading their websites and earned media coverage, reviewing their advertisements, and keeping tabs on their branding efforts. If not, you might be missing out on opportunities to differentiate your business from the others. By watching what your closest competitors are doing, you can be in a better position to maneuver your business into areas where there is a gap, filling a need not currently being met. Also, by monitoring the competition's social media, you can get a feel for what their customers like most about the business, and this can help you tweak yours to meet the expectations of clients before they even know what's happening. You don't want to be guilty of false advertising, so just make sure you can honor what you say. A professional PR agency knows what to look for when observing competitors, where to check and how to incorporate information into your PR plan in a way that is fresh and yours alone.

I hope that I've equipped you to identify how and when a PR professional can support your business growth. The eight points I've shared here are valid reasons for hiring a professional public relations expert to develop, implement, and manage an individualized PR plan for your business. Leaving all this up to chance may be the way you did business in the past, but with increased competition, new platforms which other businesses use to create awareness, and the pressure from more savvy home service businesses, it may be time to consider *next-level* help.

CHAPTER TWELVE

Partnering with the Right Specialist

Not comfortable writing about yourself and your business? Don't have time to spend on managing social media? Have no idea how to create a brand and build a reputation online? It might be in your company's best interest to hire a PR specialist. But how do you find a good one? It has to be the right one for you, someone who feels like a good fit and understands your business and your industry.

Start by calling other people in the home service industry and see if anyone can recommend a reliable and transparent PR business with a solid reputation. If you've noticed that someone in your industry is always posting on their social media about the media coverage they're getting, contact the owner and ask him about the PR agency he's using.

A word of warning: Just like there are no guarantees in your business, a PR agency can't guarantee appearances or interviews. Instead, what you want to see is examples of the campaigns they've created, and how they partner with clients to set goals and tell a specific story. If a PR agency promises a guarantee of coverage, move on. It can't be done, and it's unethical. The expert you hire should show examples of successful campaigns for a wide range of clients, including clients in your field. Those clients should have lots to say about the agency's practices and culture; they should also be able to refer to specific successes. Ask the PR agency for a few names of businesses they represent. Then look to see if those clients are receiving press coverage. Do you like what you see? Do a Google search—both of the clients and the PR agency—to learn more about the agency's practices and how effective it is at creating positive attention for its clients.

> **If a PR agency promises a guarantee of coverage, move on. It can't be done, and it's unethical.**

Once you've performed all these checks, then start making calls and see which agency meets your requirements. When you're partnering with a business, you want to make sure that your goals align and that you know you can trust them to tell your story.

A PITCH FOR THE PROS

My goal is to share the benefits of working with pros in all aspects of your business, including and especially PR. There is much more that can be accomplished by using a professional PR agency to help you develop a plan just for you. Many agencies employ professional writers who are experts in your field of business. These writers can be used to create targeted press releases, written in a style that will get published. Many writers are former journalists and have deep knowledge of your subject matter, in addition to knowing what a reporter wants. A creatively constructed press release can mean the difference between being published and being ignored. Reporters do not have time anymore to wade through superfluous content searching for the perfect story, timed to their calendar or connected to a topic of current interest. If a marketer writes your press releases, the journalist can tell, and it often gets trashed. News stations are struggling with staff cuts just like other businesses, and reporters often fill several positions. So that means the press releases needing the fewest cuts and edits are the ones that get published.

In addition to using professional writers, the best PR agencies have employees that excel at pitching stories to the right media. Pitching is also an art, and it takes experience to be good at it. Pitching involves much more than reaching out to media with a potential story. It means reading all the industry publications, watching who writes stories relevant to your industry, and understanding what they like to cover and when. It also means monitoring the editorial calendars of publications, knowing when to submit a pitch, and how to follow up without pestering. It's a delicate procedure and not for amateurs. It takes finesse, and it's not for everyone. Some reporters could take months or years before covering your story, but the PR professionals have the knowledge and the know-how to speed that process. What might take you six months to get coverage could take a few weeks using a professional.

Part of helping you tell your story involves setting that story in a larger context. In the case of PR, this means looking at things like the specific impact your business has on its community.

My clients are generous people, and we're always happy to share that part of their story with the media. We want their customers—and potential customers—to know exactly how they are giving back and sharing with the communities in which they operate.

We spend time thinking about how to partner effectively with a charity—in large part to make sure that their gift does the most good. Businesses like yours are asked for donations all the time. An employee may battle breast cancer, inspiring a request for a donation to an organization working in breast cancer research. The local Little League team may ask you for a donation to buy new uniforms for the players. A food pantry may ask for canned goods, a homeless shelter may ask for coats, an elementary school may ask for school supplies and backpacks for needy children.

These are all great causes. Please understand: I'm not saying that there is a right way and a wrong way to be generous. What I am saying is that, if you have a budget of $20,000 set aside for charitable giving, I recommend selecting one or two charities to support in a significant way. A check of $10,000 or $20,000 can make an incredible difference to these nonprofits, far more than a check of $500 to forty different organizations.

I understand the dilemma of deciding to whom and when to give. Let me share with you the strategy we use at Ripley PR. Early on, I talked with my employees about the causes that mattered to all of us. Initially, there were a lot. But as we discussed and brainstormed, we narrowed the many causes we cared about to two broad overarching areas: issues impacting children and animals. Those two areas now inform our decisions about charitable giving; the specific organizations may vary year to year, but we know that our charitable giving will involve one of those two areas.

I understand that you may feel uncomfortable linking charitable giving with PR. But here's what I tell my clients: Your company is successful enough to support this charity in two ways: first, through your donation, but also second, by shining the light on the work they're doing through PR. You can afford a PR agency; many of these nonprofits can't. They rely on volunteers to get the word out. When you publicize your donation, you're creating awareness that this nonprofit exists and highlighting the good things that they are doing. You may inspire others to donate or to volunteer their time.

And of course, it creates awareness for your company too. If you give your local animal shelter a check for $10,000, just imagine the love they'll show you on their social media pages and the impact on your business when they highlight the donation in their newsletters to supporters.

This is yet another way PR can help you tell your story. Building a legacy in your community is important. So is demonstrating that you are an organization that cares, a business whose focus is on making sure that people are comfortable and safe in their homes, and that they are living in a vibrant, healthy, flourishing community. That's a message that attracts customers. It's also a message that attracts employees.

WHAT ARE YOUR PR OPTIONS?

Businesses in the home service industry have many options when it comes to conducting public relations campaigns and promoting their business and their brand:

- Try a do-it-yourself approach

- Hire a full-time employee to run your promotional activities

- Contract with a PR agency you find online or through ads

- Engage a professional PR agency experienced in home service through referrals from noncompeting companies in your industry

The do-it-yourself approach is what many home service businesses try first. In general, this is the least effective method for getting attention for your business. The major problem with this type of marketing and PR is that business owners rarely have the time to do the job right, and are often not trained in the best ways to achieve PR.

The next step home service businesses try is hiring someone in-house to manage the promotional and marketing endeavors for their firm. This also has its drawbacks, as many businesses can't afford a top-notch PR professional, so the position is often filled by a marketing person who has good intentions but doesn't understand the media. We talked about the pros and cons of this in the last chapter, but the bottom line is that your business can end up wasting a lot of money on ineffective and poorly executed PR activities.

Still another option is to hire a PR agency as a contracted vendor from a website search or from a promotion or ad. You may get lucky and identify a skilled PR agency; however, you could end up with an agency that knows your local media but does not understand your business and has never had a home service business as a client before.

> **The future success of your business is not something to be taken lightly, so a tested, experienced, and successful home services PR agency should always be your first choice.**

Ask yourself this question: Do you want to be the test client for an agency that is supposed to be the expert in how to help you get attention, both locally and nationally, and take your business to the next level?

Of all the choices you have, the fastest and most efficient option is to hire a PR partner with years of experience in your industry. It's like the old saying: If you plan on having surgery, do want the surgeon who has done three surgeries or the one who has done three thousand?

Use the same standard of excellence and expertise that you would when choosing a potential partner or hiring an employee. Ask the key question: "What's your level of experience and how successful have you been?" This is not the time to take a chance on a novice candidate or a firm that doesn't truly understand your business, your industry, or your clients. The future success of your business is not something to be taken lightly, so a tested, experienced, and successful home services PR agency should always be your first choice.

Let me share some key criteria you'll want to consider when looking for your home services PR partner.

WHAT QUALITIES SHOULD YOUR PR PARTNER HAVE?

1. *Knowledge of your industry.*

   There are a lot of generalist agencies out there that don't have any specialties. But when it comes to home service, having knowledge about the intricacies and terminology in your industry is more important than knowledge of your local market. That's why a PR agency that specializes in the home service industry can offer more strategic help than a local PR agency currently operating in your market. You won't have to train them about what you do or the complexities and terminology specific to your business. A PR agency that has insider knowledge of home service is going to be able to tailor a PR campaign just for you, and you know your business won't be a test client for them.

2. *Clients who get substantial positive press and coverage.*

   When you see companies like yours in the news all the time, it's a good bet that they have a top-notch PR agency working on their behalf. Google the press releases the other companies put out, see who writes them for the firm, and do your research.

3. *Testimonials from happy clients.*

   Different than reviews, testimonials are recommendations from past/current clients of the PR agency that appear online, usually on the PR agency's website or the owner's LinkedIn account. These are edited versions of a client's comments about the PR agency but are generally very informative about the firm's business practices. I've said it before in connection with positive testimonials for your business; the same is absolutely true when you're choosing a PR partner. Pay attention to what their clients are saying. You can use these testimonials as a way to get to know the PR agency before contacting them.

4. *Positive stories and press for clients in trusted, respected publications.*

   Even if a PR agency's clients show up on the local news or in small, localized magazines and journals, that may not be where you want your business to show up, especially if appearing in these platforms is common for businesses like yours. What are your goals—which publications will make a difference to your strategy? Think about the places you'd like to see your business appear that really get attention: your local newspaper and television stations and specialized publications like *Contractor Magazine, Builder Magazine, ACHR News, Supply House Times*, and more.

5. *Character and chemistry.*

   Never hire a PR agency whose reputation and character do not mesh with your business culture. Whether you choose a larger firm, or a small to midsize PR partner, character matters, and how their character is communicated to you is one of the most important factors when picking the right partner. While character is critical, chemistry matters too. You want to build a trusting relationship with your partner, and for the connection to work, there has to be a meeting of the minds.

6. *The ability to tailor a PR program that is unique and just for you.*

Pay attention to what happens when you first contact a potential PR partner. If the PR agency doesn't respond quickly, or if it makes you feel like a small fish in a very big pond, that firm may not be a good match for you. While you want a top-notch PR partner, you also don't want to get lost in the shuffle. Make sure that they won't take a one-size-fits-all approach to your campaign; you want ideas that are targeted and that help you distinguish your business from its competitors.

7. *Contracts that fit your budget and style.*

If you find that perfect PR agency, go through all the research, due diligence, and fact finding, you'll undoubtedly feel relieved and excited. But there's still one more key step: if you get to the contract stage and are confused or unsure about what you are really getting for your money, don't rush into signing. Look for a PR partner that wants to create a win-win relationship and is willing to take the time to explain the process to you before you sign on the dotted line.

WHAT YOU CAN BRING TO THIS RELATIONSHIP

Now that we have covered what to look for in a PR agency, it's a good time to talk about what you, the client, needs to bring to the table.

Which qualities are important for a good PR client to possess?

I've spent a lot of time meeting with business owners, C-Suite executives, marketing directors, franchisees, franchisors, and everything in between. That experience has led me to one clear conclusion: an informed client makes the best client.

I want you to be that informed client. So here are a few key goals I suggest that you spend some time reflecting on. Be clear about each of these, and bring them with you to your first meeting with your potential PR partner.

1. *Have a budget in mind.*

   This is important, and not just because a PR agency is interested in getting your business from a financial point of view. A PR agency should be ready to support your goals, including those for your budget. In fact, we'd rather work within your actual budget than plan a meticulous PR program that is not realistic for your business. Most reputable PR agencies can accommodate many budgets, and we can explain these options if you are clear about your budget and expectations from the beginning.

2. *Embrace the relationship as a partnership.*

   Your PR agency of choice will do a lot to get you the media attention you need to take your business to the next level. But we also need you and your employees to think of us as an extension of your team. Your total commitment to this new endeavor can make all the difference in the success of our efforts on your behalf.

3. *Be ready when we set up a media opportunity.*

   This sounds silly, doesn't it? But it happens more than you

would think. I remember a client many years ago who said he wanted to be interviewed by *The Wall Street Journal* at almost every monthly meeting. He worked diligently and with a laser focus to get that opportunity, and after much back and forth with the reporter, I was successful! I was thrilled as I informed my client that there was an interview with their media outlet of choice, and I expected my client to be every bit as excited as I was. But he hesitated and said that he needed time to think about whether he could do it and what he would say. He missed the chance by responding too late. At that point, the reporter was no longer interested in that client or the story. The moral here is this: It's not easy to get coverage in a major (or any) publication, so if you get an opportunity, don't waste it.

4. *Be willing to take chances.*

It can seem scary to take chances with your business—to test out new ways of promoting your work and your mission, and to trust someone else to effectively tell your story. Keep this in mind: if you don't do anything different, you'll never have a different outcome. It is said that Thomas Edison failed 1,000 times when creating the light bulb. But if he had not tried 1,001 times, who knows how long it would have taken someone else to have the idea? The point here is that it's natural to feel a little nervous about trying something new. It *should* feel different. Everything new is a chance, but it could be the chance that makes a world of difference.

5. *Share your dreams.*

This may be the most important aspect of working with a PR agency. To make the magic happen, we need to be in on the secrets. As your partner, your PR agency can only work with what it is told, and if your business goals are a secret, your PR agency is working at a disadvantage. The relationship is like any other in your life, and that means that honesty is crucial. So share your business goals. Discuss the new ventures you're planning. Talk about the good you are doing and the challenges you're facing, and be prepared to have a partner that believes in you as much as you do.

I said it at the beginning of this book: public relations involves building good relationships. And that includes the relationship with your PR partner.

Choose that partner wisely. Be clear about your expectations, be realistic about your budget, be open about your goals, and be willing to consider a fresh approaches and new opportunities to reach your customers.

CONCLUSION

PR isn't just about press and media attention. It's about telling the story of your business—a story that lets the world know that your business exists, that it's a business with value and good people and quality work. It's about helping get your website on page one of a Google search, building recognition of your brand, and ensuring that your reputation is strong. It's about embracing and celebrating what is unique and significant about your business and equipping you to meet challenges quickly and effectively. It means embracing the opportunities that will help you increase your revenue and take your business to the next level.

That next level might be to reach a million dollars in revenue, or to increase from one million to three million. Your next level might be to move from three to five million, or from ten to twenty.

To make that leap—to move to the next level now—you need to do things differently. You need to market your business differently and speak in a different way to customers and potential customers.

PR can be that step—that fresh approach that can propel your business to that next level you are ready to reach.

My goal as a PR professional is to serve my clients and serve their industry. I hope that this book has demonstrated the value of the work

I do and how it can benefit the work that you do.

Every day, I partner with home service business owners, equipping them to think strategically about how PR can support their goals. I'd love to have that same conversation with you.

So do your research. Visit my website: prsecretsforhomeservice.com. Take a look at the work that we do.

If you like what you see, if you're inspired to take your business to the next level, give me a call. I'm happy to give you a free thirty-minute consultation on how PR can benefit your business.

Whatever your goals for your business, I want to help you achieve them. I want you to have new opportunities to tell your company's story, to highlight your services, to demonstrate your expertise.

I believe in the value of the work you do. I want you to be successful. And I know that public relations can help you grow your business to the next level.

ACKNOWLEDGMENTS

Growing up with family members who worked in the trades helped me understand and have a special affinity for home service and skilled tradesmen and women. But it wasn't until years after building a career in marketing that I found my calling while working with Clockwork Home Services, the parent company of the successful One Hour Heating & Air Conditioning, Mister Sparky, and Benjamin Franklin Plumbing franchises. The people I worked with, especially the franchise owners, made a profound impact on me and my decision to start my own PR agency specializing in the home service industry.

Clockwork was my introduction to home service marketing and PR, but it was the business owners who fueled the fire inside me. They helped me learn even more about the industry, and it is their enthusiasm and entrepreneurial spirit that keep me striving even more. I wish I had the room to thank every person who has touched my life, made an impression, taught me, and encouraged me.

From past employees to current ones, and even some of my competitors, so many wonderful individuals have believed in and supported my vision and have influenced the paths I have taken. Throughout the ups and downs of my own business and personal life, so many have stayed the course and offered their support.

On my recent path to attain greater calm and healthier habits, I have developed a love for martial arts. A huge thank you to my Brazilian Jiu-Jitsu instructor, Professor Jerry Burns. His instruction and patience have helped balance my brain and calm my nonstop thoughts about running a business.

Without all these people, Ripley PR wouldn't be where it is, and I wouldn't have been able to write this book.

So many people have inspired my journey that there's no way I can remember all the names, so this is a BIG THANK YOU for your coaching and support along the way, and if I forgot anyone, please allow me to say I'm sorry by buying you a beer!

Jim Abrams

Charles Bonfiglio

Tab Burkhalter

Stephen Christopher

Michael Corley

Rocco DiBenedetto

Brigham Dickinson

Jaime DiDomenico

Ashley Dooley

Jerry Hall

Joe Haniford

Michelle Hogan

Sarah Horvath

Tab Hunter

Rodney Koop

Vahe Kuzoyan

Bob Mader

Ara Mahdessian

Bill Mattern

Bill McPherson

Jim Nichols

Terry Nicholson

Michael Petri

Danielle Putnam

Ted Puzio

Bryan Richards

Ellen Rohr

Andy Ryan

Steve Smith

Denise Swafford

Bruce Wiseman

John Young

ABOUT THE AUTHOR

Heather Ripley is passionate about helping business owners in the skilled trades embrace the power of public relations to grow. Over her career, she's helped hundreds of contractors boost their visibility and reputation.

Heather cares deeply about the people in the home service industry, people who keep our great nation running. She believes that these men and women are heroes who make sure that their customers' homes are safe, comfortable, and healthy every day.

Growing up in a blue-collar family, Heather learned about the worth and dignity of the trades early on. Her father was an automotive collision technician, and her grandfather was a truck driver. Going even further back, her great-grandfather was an electrician for South Carolina Power & Light.

Heather got her start managing marketing for all three of the Clockwork Home Services brands, earning the company top-tier media exposure, including an appearance on *The Celebrity Apprentice* in 2009. She has worked with hundreds of contractors, both at Clockwork and through her own agency, Ripley PR.

Heather founded Ripley PR in her hometown of Maryville, Tennessee. A global public relations agency specializing in skilled trades, B2B, and franchising, Ripley PR was named by *Forbes* as one of America's Best PR Agencies in 2021, and recognized by *Entrepreneur* magazine as a Top Franchise PR Agency three years in a row. Heather is also a regular contributor to *PHC News*.